Understanding Artificial Intelligence

Understanding Artificial Intelligence

Fundamentals and Applications

Albert Chun Chen Liu
Kneron Inc,
San Diego, USA

Oscar Ming Kin Law
Kneron Inc,
San Diego, USA

Iain Law
University of California,
San Diego, USA

IEEE PRESS

WILEY

Published by John Wiley & Sons, Inc., Hoboken, New Jersey.
Published simultaneously in Canada.

For general information on our other products and services or for technical support, please contact our Customer Care Department within the United States at (800) 762-2974, outside the United States at (317) 572-3993 or fax (317) 572-4002.

Wiley also publishes its books in a variety of electronic formats. Some content that appears in print may not be available in electronic formats. For more information about Wiley products, visit our website at www.wiley.com.

Library of Congress Cataloging-in-Publication Data
Names: Liu, Albert Chun Chen, author. | Law, Oscar Ming Kin, author. | Law, Iain, author.
Title: Understanding artificial intelligence : fundamentals and applications / Albert Chun Chen Liu, Oscar Ming Kin Law, Iain Law.
Description: Hoboken, New Jersey : Wiley-IEEE Press, [2022] | Includes bibliographical references and index.
Identifiers: LCCN 2022017564 (print) | LCCN 2022017565 (ebook) | ISBN 9781119858331 (cloth) | ISBN 9781119858348 (adobe pdf) | ISBN 9781119858386 (epub)
Subjects: LCSH: Artificial intelligence.
Classification: LCC Q335 .L495 2022 (print) | LCC Q335 (ebook) | DDC 006.3–dc23/eng20220718
LC record available at https://lccn.loc.gov/2022017564
LC ebook record available at https://lccn.loc.gov/2022017565

Cover Design: Wiley
Cover Image: © Blue Planet Studio/Shutterstock

Set in 9.5/12.5pt STIXTwoText by Straive, Pondicherry, India

Printed in the United States of America

Education is not the learning of facts,
but the training of the mind to think

Albert Einstein

Contents

List of Figures

Preface

This book is inspired by the Chinese Christian Herald Crusades (Los Angles), Youth Enrichment and Leadership Program (YELP) – "AI Workshops." It introduces the youth to the fourth industrial revolution (Industrial Revolution 4.0) – artificial intelligence (AI) technology. The industrial revolution started with the steam engine (1784), electricity (1870), the computer (1969), to the latest AI technology (2012) – neural network. AI combines the neural network with big data (BD) and the internet of things (IoT), which dramatically changes our everyday life. Today, autonomous vehicles (Tesla), virtual assistants (Google Home), and drone delivery (Amazon Prime Air) are all supported by AI. With AI advances, it displaces million and generates more jobs in the near future. History repeats itself, data entry replaced the typist, but data entry offered more job opportunities at the beginning of the computer era. The book shows the readers how to face AI challenges. It explains basic neural network architecture, machine vision, natural language processing (NLP), autonomous vehicle, and drone technologies. It also covers AI developments, healthcare, finance, retail, manufacturing, agriculture, smart city, and government. Finally, it also describes the different hardware designs targeted for AI applications.

The book is organized as follows:

- Chapter 1 describes the AI history and its impact on our world. It shows how the neural network is derived from the human neuron and highlights the popular neural network architectures, convolutional neural network (CNN), recurrent neural network (RNN), and reinforcement learning (RL). Based on the neural network training mechanism, it classifies the networks into supervised learning, semi-supervised learning, and unsupervised learning. It also discusses two primary neural network operations, training and inference.
- Chapter 2 introduces the classical CNN architecture. It briefly explains the primary functional layers, convolutional layer, activation layer, pooling layer, batch normalization, dropout, and fully connected layer.

- Chapter 3 describes the machine vision approach. It focuses on object recognition, especially facial recognition. It explains how to recognize the object through deep convolution neural network (DCNN) and evolve the small feature maps into complete object images. It covers the major machine vision applications in medical diagnosis, retail applications, and airport security.

- Chapter 4 explains how to apply AI for NLP. It focuses on various neural network architectures, CNN, RNN with long-short term memory (LSTM), recursive neural network, and RL. It describes the NLP applications, virtual assistants, language translation, and text transcription.

- Chapter 5 introduces the autonomous vehicle, also called the self-driving car. It lists the autonomous vehicle standard based on the Society of Automotive Engineers (SAE) International. It describes various autonomous technologies, computer vision, sensor fusion, localization, path finding, drive control, communication strategies, vehicle-to-vehicle, vehicle-to-infrastructure, and vehicle-to-pedestrian. It also discusses the autonomous vehicle law legislation and future challenges.

- Chapter 6 introduces the unmanned aerial vehicle (UAV) – drone development. It explores drone designs, applications, and challenges. It lists out both recreational and commercial rules initialized by Federal Aviation Administration (FAA). Finally, it covers the popular drone applications in civil construction, agriculture, and emergence rescue.

- Chapter 7 describes artificial intelligence's impacts on the healthcare system. It includes telemedicine, medical diagnosis, medical imaging, smart medical devices, electronic health records, medical billing, drug development, clinical trial, medical robotics, and elderly care. It also highlights the challenges of AI in the healthcare system.

- Chapter 8 shows how to integrate AI in finance sectors and explores the impacts on fraud detection, financial forecast, stock trading, financial advisory, accounting, and insurance.

- Chapter 9 highlights important changes in future retail, such as e-commerce, virtual shopping, promotion optimization, store management, warehouse management, and supply chain. It also shows the next-generation retail store, the Amazon Go store.

- Chapter 10 describes the AI impacts on manufacturing. It covers defect detection, quality assurance, generative design, predictive maintenance, environment sustainability, and manufacturing optimization. AI dramatically improves overall productivity.

- Chapter 11 lists the changes in agriculture, crop and soil monitoring, agricultural robot, pest control, and precision farming. It shows how to apply AI to reduce the labor demand and increase productivity in agriculture.

- Chapter 12 shows smart city development. It covers smart transportation, smart parking, waste management, smart grid, and environmental health. Currently, New York and Taipei rank the world's top 10 smart cities.
- Chapter 13 describes how the government faces AI challenges, including information technology, human service, law enforcement, legislation, and ethics. It also covers the public perspective toward AI.
- Chapter 14 shows various AI computational platforms, central processing unit (CPU) – Intel, graphical processing unit (GPU) – Nvidia, tensor processing unit (TPU) – Google, and neural processing unit (NPU) – Kneron.

The book also provides the software laboratories, which lets the reader further understand the AI concept using the neural network model Yolo v3 for object detection. The reader can develop different applications using Kneron NPU. The optional Yolo v5[1] example is introduced to improve the object detection performance.

The laboratories are listed as follows:

- Laboratory 1 shows how to install Python and its libraries with Kneron NPU to perform image/video object detection.
- Laboratory 2 describes how to apply Kneron NPU (hardware accelerator) to speed up object detection.
- Laboratory 3 compares the object detection performance using Kneron NPU with different transfer modes: serial, pipeline, and parallel transfer.
- Laboratory 4 provides optional Yolo v5 examples to enhance object detection performance. However, it required additional Nvidia GPU and Microsoft VC++ support for model compilation.

---

1 Yolo v5 is released in June 2020.

Acknowledgments

We would like to thank all who have supported the book publishing. Thank you for the Chinese Christian Herald Crusades (Los Angles), Youth Enrichment, and Leadership Program (YELP). Many thanks to Kidd Su and Enoch Law for hardware and software project development. We also thank Raymond Tsui for smart drone support. We especially thank Claire Chang and Charlene Jin for managing the book production. Finally, we would like to thank our families for their support during the book publishing.

Author Biographies

Albert Chun Chen Liu, Kneron's founder and CEO. After graduating from the Taiwan National Cheng Kung University, he got scholarships from Raytheon and the University of California to join the UC Berkeley/UCLA/UCSD research programs and then earned his PhD in electrical engineering from the University of California Los Angeles (UCLA). Before establishing Kneron in San Diego in 2015, he worked in R&D and management positions in Qualcomm, Samsung Electronics R&D center, MStar, and Wireless Information.

Albert has been invited to give lectures on computer vision technology and artificial intelligence at the University of California and be a technical reviewer for many internationally renowned academic journals. Also, he owned more than 30 international patents in artificial intelligence, computer vision, and image processing. He has published more than 70 papers in major international journals. He is a recipient of the IEEE TCAS Darlington award in 2021.

Oscar Ming Kin Law is the director of engineering at Kneron, who works on autonomous vehicle development and new compute-in-memory (CIM) architecture. He has worked at ATI, AMD, TSMC, and Qualcomm for physical verification, library development, signal integrity, power analysis, Design for Manufacturability (DFM), and advanced technology evaluation. He received his Ph.D. from the University of Toronto, Canada.

He has published multiple artificial intelligence textbooks and over 70 patents in various areas of his field. He has also conducted seminars at UCLA, UCSD, SDSU, BYU, UT (Canada), Qualcomm, and TSMC.

Iain Law studies Economics and data science at the University of California, San Diego. In high school, he was successful in Public Forum debates, serving as the team's Vice President and qualifying for the National Tournament of Champions. Moreover, he is passionate about artificial intelligence and its impacts on the youth, working on several artificial intelligence projects like the LEGO smart robot and DJI Tello smart drone. He has also helped run the AI Workshop under the Herald YELP program, which introduces new artificial intelligence concepts to the youth. Currently, he is preparing an AI workshop series (Spanish) for STEM education, revealing how to face future artificial intelligence challenges.

1

Introduction

1.1 Overview

The rise of new artificial intelligence (AI) technology – neural network (NN) starts the fourth industrial revolution (Industry 4.0) [1, 2, 3] (Figure 1.1). The industrial revolution began with the steam engine replacing the workforce with machine and mechanized production. In the late nineteenth century, electricity modernized the world through light bulbs, telephone, and television. It led to mass industrial production. The computer bought other digital revolution to automate production and improve our lives. The fourth industrial revolution transforms the digital world into an intelligent era with the NN. Compared with the traditional approach, algorithmic programming is no longer required. A large amount of structured or unstructured data is directly fed into the NN, which automatically identifies, classifies, and predicts results. Combining AI with big data (BD), and the internet of things (IoT) completely changes our everyday life, such as autonomous vehicles (Tesla), voice assistants (Google Home), and drone delivery (Amazon Prime Air).

What is AI? AI is divided into three different levels: AI, machine learning (ML), and deep learning (DL) (Figure 1.2).

- AI is first proposed in the 1950s, which enables the computer to emulate human intelligence to solve the problem.
- ML is the subset of AI, which teaches the computer to learn and make decisions.
- DL is the subset of machine learning, which extracts the object features through a large amount of data, then identifies and classifies the information.

In 2012, University of Toronto researchers proposed convolutional neural network (CNN) – AlexNet [4] to win the ImageNet Large Scale Visual Recognition

Understanding Artificial Intelligence: Fundamentals and Applications, First Edition.
Albert Chun Chen Liu, Oscar Ming Kin Law, and Iain Law.
© 2022 The Institute of Electrical and Electronics Engineers, Inc.
Published 2022 by John Wiley & Sons, Inc.

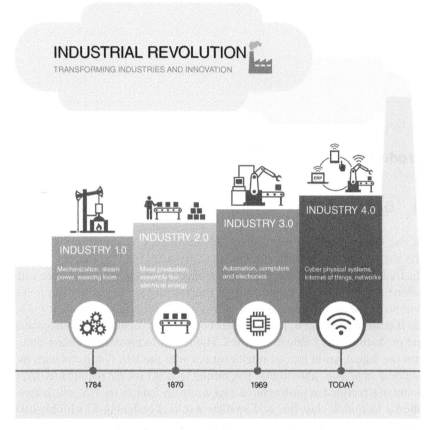

Figure 1.1 Fourth industrial revolution [3]. Source: elenabsl/Adobe Stock.

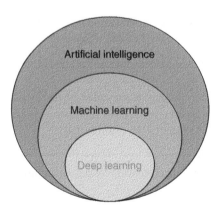

Figure 1.2 Artificial intelligence.

Challenge (ILSVRC 2012). It successfully identified the object, and the top 5% error rate is 10% less than traditional computer vision algorithmic programming. It is an important milestone in AI development. Based on CNNs, different NN models are rapidly developed for various applications. For less than five years, ResNet has shown a less than 5% error rate for object identification in ILSVRC 2015, which is better than the human accurate level. In 2016, Google AlphaGo won the GO world Champion through reinforcement learning (RL), which is the other NN breakthrough. AlphaGo reacts differently to every move in the GO game to maximize the win's chance. RL further enables smart robot automation in the manufacturing industry.

AI is currently widely applied to our everyday lives, healthcare, finance, retail, manufacturing, agriculture, smart city, and government. Tesla autopilot guides the driver for lane changes, navigating interchanges, and highway exits. It will support traffic sign recognition and autonomous driving in the city soon. Besides the machine vision applications, Google Home applies natural language processing (NLP) approach to control home appliances, play music, and answer simple questions. Amazon Prime Air[1] uses drones to deliver small packages in rural areas. It dramatically reduces the delivery cost and saves time.

AI will displace 75 million jobs but generate 133 million new ones worldwide by 2022. Like the typist was replaced by data entry in the computer era, the data entry creates more job opportunities. The book shows the readers how to prepare for new challenges.

1.2 Development History

Neural network [5] had been developed for a long time (Figure 1.3). In 1943, the first computer electronic numerical integrator and calculator (ENIAC) was constructed at the University of Pennsylvania. At the same time, neurophysiologist,

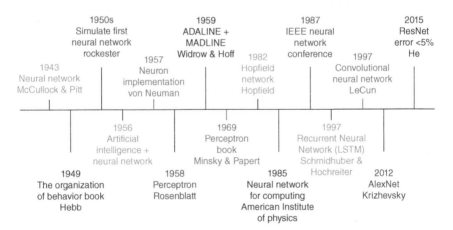

Figure 1.3 Neural network development timeline. Source: Republished with permission Liu and Law [16], permission conveyed through Copyright Clearance Center, Inc.

---

1 Amazon Prime Air received Federal Aviation Administration (FAA) approval for package delivery using unmanned aerial vehicle, drone in August 2020.

Warren McCulloch, and a mathematician, Walter Pitts, described how neurons might work [6] and modeled a simple NN using an electrical circuit. In 1949, Donald Hebb wrote the book, *The Organization of Behavior*, which pointed out how the NN is strengthened through practice.

In the 1950s, Nathanial Rochester simulated the first NN in IBM Research Laboratory. In 1956, the Dartmouth Summer Research Project on Artificial Intelligence linked AI with NNs for joint project development. In the following year, John von Neumann suggested implementing simple neuron functions using telegraph relays or vacuum tubes. A neurobiologist from Cornell University, Frank Rosenblatt, worked on Perceptron [7], a single-layer perceptron to classify the two classes' results. The perception computes the weighted sum of the inputs and subtracts a threshold, then outputs one of two possible outcomes. Perception is the oldest NN model still used today. However, Marvin Minsky and Seymour Papert published the book, *Perceptron* [8], to show the limitation of perception in 1969.

In 1959, Bernard Widrow and Marcian Hoff from Stanford University developed Multiple ADaptive LINear Elements called ADALINE and MADALINE, which were adaptive filters to eliminate the echoes in the phone line. Due to unmatured electronics and fear of the machine's impacts on humans, NN development was halted for a decade.

Until 1982, John Hopfield presented a new NN model, the Hopfield NN [9], in the National Academy of Sciences. At the same time, the United States started to fund NN research to compete with Japan after Japan announced fifth-generation AI research in US–Japan Cooperative/Competitive Neural Networks joint conference. In 1985, the American Institute of Physics started the annual meeting, Neural Network for Computing. By 1987, the first IEEE Neural Network International Conference took place with 1800 attendees. In 1997, Schmidhuber and Hochreiter proposed a recurrent NN model with long-short term memory (LSTM) useful for future time series speech processing. In 1997, Yann LeCun published *Gradient-Based Learning Applied to Document Recognition* [10], which introduced the CNN that laid the foundation for modern deep NN development.

During ImageNet Large Scale Visual Recognition Challenge (ILSVRC 2012) [11], University of Toronto researchers applied the deep convolutional neural network (DCNN) model, AlexNet [4], successfully recognized the object and achieved a top-5 error rate 10% better than traditional computer vision algorithmic approaches. For ILSVRC, there are over 14 million images with 21,000 classes and more than 1 million images with bounding boxes. The competition focused on 1000 classes with a trimmed database for image classification and object detection. For image classification, the class label is assigned to the object in the images, and it localizes the object with a bounding box for object detection. With the

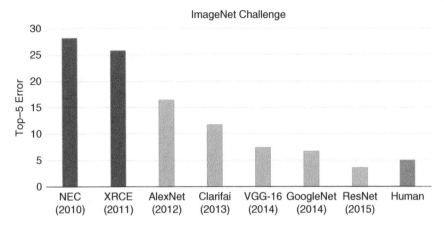

Figure 1.4 ImageNet challenge. Source: Republished with permission Liu and Law [16], permission conveyed through Copyright Clearance Center, Inc.

evolution of deep NN models, Clarifia [12], VGG-16 [13], GoogleNet [14], the error rate was rapidly reduced. In 2015, ResNet [15] showed an error rate of less than 5% human-level accuracy. The rapid growth of deep learning is transforming our world (Figure 1.4).

1.3 Neural Network Model

The NN models the neuron in the human brain. The brain consists of 86 billion neurons, and each neuron has a cell body (or soma), which controls the function of the neuron. Dendrites are branch-like structures extending away from the cell body responsible for neuron communication. It receives the message from other neurons and allows the message to travel to the cell body. An axon carries an electric impulse from the cell body to the opposite end of the neuron. The axon terminal passes the impulse to another neuron. The synapse is the chemical junction between the axon terminal and other dendrites where the chemical reaction occurs. It decides how to transmit the message between the neurons through excited and inhibited operations. The neuron allows the brain to send the message to the rest of the body and control all body actions.

The NN consists of the node, weight, and activation (Figure 1.5). The node (cell body) controls the network function and performs the computation. The weight (axon) connects to a single node or multiple ones for signal transfer. The activation (synapse) decides the signal transfer from one node to another.

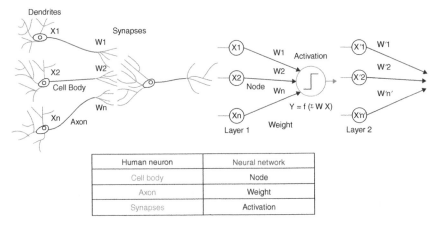

Figure 1.5 Human neuron and neural network comparison. Source: Republished with permission Liu and Law [16], permission conveyed through Copyright Clearance Center, Inc.

1.4 Popular Neural Network

This chapter introduces three popular NN models: CNN, recurrent neural network (RNN), and RL.

1.4.1 Convolutional Neural Network

CNN (Figure 1.6) is widely used for object classification and detection. It consists of the input, output, and multiple hidden layers. The image and video are first fed into the input layer for neural processing. The hidden layers consist of the

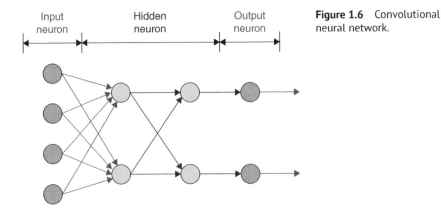

Figure 1.6 Convolutional neural network.

convolutional, activation, pooling, dropout, and fully connected layers. The convolutional layer extracts the object features and evolves the features from simple to complex. The activation layer filters out the non-existence features and eliminates unnecessary operations. The pooling layer simplifies the computations and keeps the reasonable feature size. It predicts the results using the fully connected layer. The CNN is further divided into DCNN, region-based convolutional neural network (RCNN), fast-region-based neural network (Fast-RCNN), faster-region-based neural network (Faster-RCNN), and Yolo models. Except for the DCNN, all other models identify the object and provide a bounding box to show the object size and position. It is widely used for autonomous vehicles.

1.4.2 Recurrent Neural Network

RNN (Figure 1.7) targets NLP, and the architecture is similar to the CNN. The language is made up of words, and they are related to others, called times series. The data is fed to the RNN sequentially for computation. A modified LSTM with additional memory stores the current and previous inputs. It can improve the accuracy of language processing. The common RNN includes the LSTM network, Hopfield network, and bidirectional associative network (BAM). LSTM network is usually integrated with voice assistants, such as Google Home and Amazon Alexa.

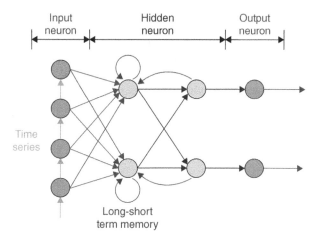

Figure 1.7 Recurrent neural network.

1.4.3 Reinforcement Learning

RL (Figure 1.8) is different from the CNN, consisting of agents and the environment. Depending on the current state and environmental changes. The agent reacts differently to maximize the accumulative reward. RL is widely applied to

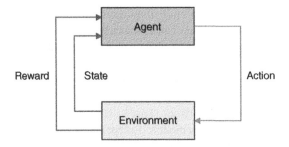

Figure 1.8 Reinforcement learning.

video game design and robotic control. The typical RL includes the deep Q network (DQN) and asynchronous advantage actor-critic (A3C).

1.5 Neural Network Classification

The NN is divided into supervised, semi-supervised, and unsupervised learning based on the training mechanism.

1.5.1 Supervised Learning

Supervised learning sets the target and trains with a particular input dataset to minimize the error between the expected and predicted results. After the training, the network can successfully predict the results for the unknown inputs. The popular supervised models are CNN and RNN, which includes the LSTM network.

Regression (Figure 1.9) is typically used for supervised learning; it finds the relationship between the input and output and predicts the value based on the input dataset. The common regression is Linear Regression (LR).

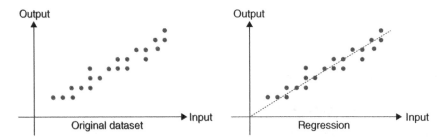

Figure 1.9 Regression. Source: Republished with permission Liu and Law [16], permission conveyed through Copyright Clearance Center, Inc.

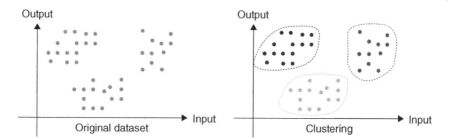

Figure 1.10 Clustering.

1.5.2 Semi-supervised Learning

Semi-supervised learning is based on partial labeled output for training, where RL is the best example. Unlabeled data is mixed with a small amount of labeled data can improve the learning accuracy under different environments.

1.5.3 Unsupervised Learning

Unsupervised learning is the network that learns the important features from the dataset, which exploits the relationship among the inputs through clustering, dimensionality reduction, and generative techniques. The examples include auto encoder (AE), restricted Boltzmann machine (RBM), and deep belief network (DBN).

Clustering (Figure 1.10) is a useful technique for unsupervised learning. It divides the dataset into multiple groups where the data points are similar to each other in the same group. The popular clustering algorithm is the k-means technique.

1.6 Neural Network Operation

The NN operation is mainly divided into two primary operations: training and inference.

1.6.1 Training

As a human being, it takes time to train the NN to recognize the object's features. Training feeds the dataset into the NN, and the network parameters are updated to minimize the error between the desired and predicted outputs. Training is a computationally intensive procedure and applies floating-point computation to enhance accuracy. It takes a few hours to a few days to train the network using cloud computing or high-performance computing (HPC) processors.

1.6.2 Inference

Once the training is completed, the trained NN can predict the results; this operation is called inference. It only takes a few seconds to a minute for prediction. Most of the deep learning accelerators are optimized for inference in embedded applications, especially for the IoT. It simplifies the computation using the fixed-point calculation and skips the zero elements through network pruning to speed up the overall operations.

1.7 Application Development

This chapter describes the AI application development cycle (Figure 1.11), from business planning, network design, data engineering, and validation to final deployment. It not only solves the technical problems but also considers the human factor. It tries to minimize the machine–human conflicts. This approach has been successfully applied for healthcare, finance, retail, manufacturing, agriculture, smart city, and government (Figure 1.12).

1.7.1 Business Planning

For application development, the business analysts first develop the AI vision, understands the problem, benefit, and technology trade-off, then define the long-term AI investment strategy. The analysts not only focus on technical issues but also consider the company culture, the personnel, and management, then decide how to integrate AI into the current business environment. During the

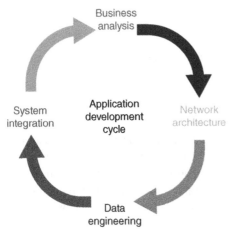

Figure 1.11 Application development cycle.

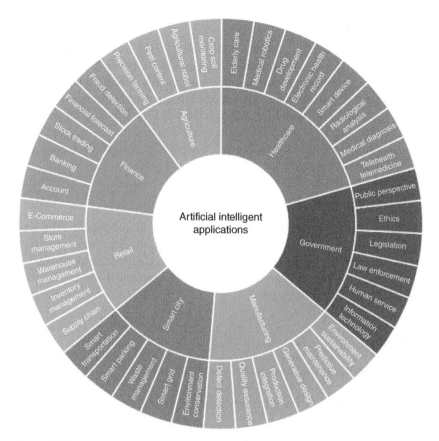

Figure 1.12 Artificial intelligence applications.

development, they should offer the employees the training program to adopt AI in the working environment. Moreover, the analysts work with the developers to define the system specification, the migration requirements, and the performance measure. The analysts also monitor the development progress for future improvement.

1.7.2 Network Design

The AI architects work with business analysts to understand the problems and requirements. They explore various approaches and different NN architectures. After the preliminary evaluation, the architects choose the best NN architecture for implementation. The architects also define the input criteria and desired output, then refine the design to achieve optimal performance.

1.7.3 Data Engineering

The data engineers collect the structural and nonstructural data, then translate them into the correct format for model training. They are also responsible for optimizing the computationally intensive training process and reducing the training time. It is easy to feed the data into training to improve the model accuracy. The engineers also validate the output results with the design specification for accurate prediction.

Moreover, the engineers update the model subjected to the evaluation feedback and the requirement changes. The engineers also modify the NN to improve the overall performance further.

1.7.4 System Integration

The system engineers finally integrate the application into the business environment through the user-friendly human-machine interface. The engineers make sure the AI applications are fully compatible with other business applications. They are responsible for daily operations and update the system based on the users' feedback. Finally, they send feedback to the developers for future enhancement.

Exercise

1. How do the industrial revolutions change the world?

2. How do you describe the difference between AI, ML, and DL?

3. Why do people fear the rise of AI?

4. Should we worry about the sentient AI?

5. What are AI impacts on healthcare, finance, retail, manufacturing, agriculture, smart city, and government?

6. How does AI affect the future job market?

7. How does the NN derive from the human neuron?

8. What are the three popular NNs and their functions?

9. How do you classify the NN with examples?

10. What are the NN basic operations, training, and inference?

11. How do you develop AI applications?

2

Neural Network

This chapter introduces the classical neural network model, AlexNet [4, 16] (Figure 2.1), consisting of eight network layers. The first five layers are the convolutional layer with the nonlinear activation layer, rectified linear unit (ReLU). It is followed by the max-pooling layer to reduce the kernel size and the local response normalization (LRN) layer to improve the computation stability. The last three layers are fully connected layers for object classification.

The deeper and wider neural network model allows the simple features to evolve to the complete one [17] and achieves better prediction (Figure 2.2). The drawback of deep learning is the computation intensity. It is required to perform billions of operations to update the model parameters. Therefore, Kneron neural processing unit (NPU) is introduced in laboratories. It converts the floating-point operations to the fixed point one, prunes the network, and skips the ineffectual zero operations to speed up the inference.

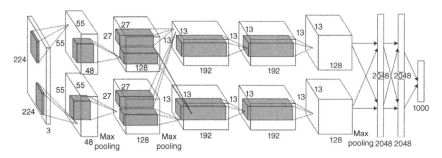

Figure 2.1 Convolutional neural network architecture. Source: Krizhevsky et al. [4] / with permission of ACM, Inc.

Understanding Artificial Intelligence: Fundamentals and Applications, First Edition.
Albert Chun Chen Liu, Oscar Ming Kin Law, and Iain Law.
© 2022 The Institute of Electrical and Electronics Engineers, Inc.
Published 2022 by John Wiley & Sons, Inc.

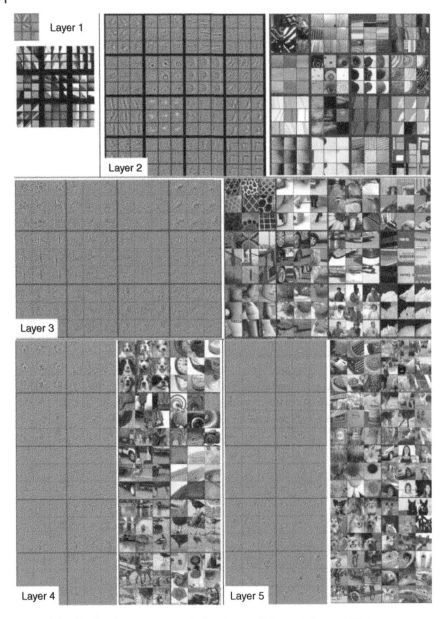

Figure 2.2 AlexNet feature map evolution. Source: Zeiler and Fergus [17] / Springer Nature.

2.1   Convolutional Layer

The convolutional layer targets object feature extraction through convolution (Figure 2.3). The input image (called input feature map) is convolved with the filter to extract the object features across all the image channels.[1] The filter slides through the image pixel, multiplies the corresponding image pixel, and sums the results together. The process is repeated until all image pixels are processed. The input image is processed together as a batch to improve the filter reuse. The output is called output feature maps. For some network models, the bias offset is introduced with zero paddings for edge filtering without the feature size reduction. The stride is designed for the sliding window to avoid the large output feature maps.

$$Y = X \otimes W \tag{2.1}$$

$$y_{i,j} = \sum_{m=0}^{M-1} \sum_{n=0}^{N-1} x_{m,n} w_{i-m,j-n} \tag{2.2}$$

where

y is the output feature map
x is the input image
w is the filter weight

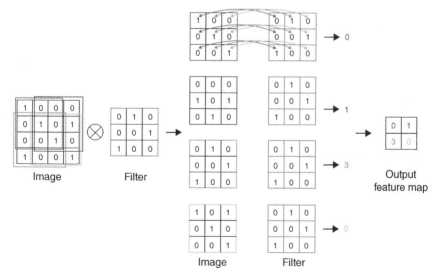

Figure 2.3   Image convolution. Source: Republished with permission of Liu and Law [16], permission conveyed through Copyright Clearance Center, Inc.

---

1 The image pixel is typically represented by the basic color, R(ed), G(reen), B(lue) in three different image channels.

2.2 Activation Layer

$$y = \max(0, x) \tag{2.3}$$

where

y is the activation output
x is the activation input

A nonlinear activation layer (also called threshold function) (Figure 2.4) is applied after the convolutional or fully connected layer. It rectifies the negative convolutional results and sets them to zero. The negative convolutional results mean that the extracted features do not exist and introduce the network sparsity. Network sparsity is critical for neural processing; it wastes the computational resource to calculate the zero results. Therefore, the network pruning and ineffectual skipping approaches are widely used to eliminate the zero operations, which speeds up the overall computation. There are various nonlinear activation functions, and ReLU is the most popular one.

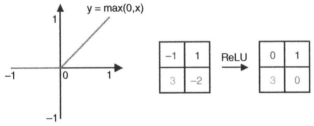

Rectified linear unit (ReLU)

Figure 2.4 Activation function. Source: Republished with permission of Liu and Law [16], permission conveyed through Copyright Clearance Center, Inc.

2.3 Pooling Layer

$$\text{Max pooling} \quad y = \max\left(x_{mn}\right) \tag{2.4}$$

$$\text{Average pooling} \quad y = \frac{1}{MN} \sum_{m=0}^{M-1} \sum_{n=0}^{N-1} x_{m,n} \tag{2.5}$$

where

y is the pooling output
x is the pooling input

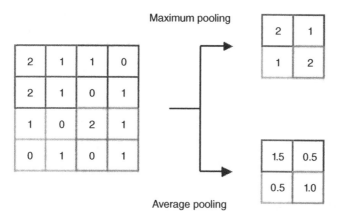

Figure 2.5 Pooling layer. Source: Republished with permission of Liu and Law [16], permission conveyed through Copyright Clearance Center, Inc.

Pooling reduces the feature maps' dimension, making the network more robust and invariant to the small shifts and variations. The pooling is further divided into the maximum and average pooling (Figure 2.5). The maximum pooling chooses the maximum from the group of inputs, and the average pooling is the average from all the values. The maximum is preferred over the average because it can distinguish the small features in the input feature maps.

2.4 Batch Normalization

The layer output feeds to the next layer input affecting the covariance shift and causally relates to prediction accuracy. Batch normalization (BN) is used to control the input distortion with zero mean and unit standard deviation. It makes the network more robust to the weight initialization and the covariance shift through normalizing and scaling. It also speeds up the training with higher accuracy. Currently, the BN replaces the original LRN, where the normalization can be further scaled and shifted.

2.5 Dropout Layer

During the training, the dropout layer (Figure 2.6) randomly ignores the activation to prevent the overfitting problem by reducing the neuron correlation.

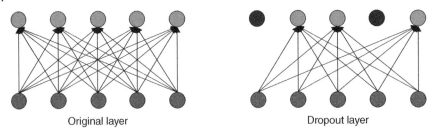

Original layer   Dropout layer

Figure 2.6 Dropout layer. Source: Republished with permission of Liu and Law [16], permission conveyed through Copyright Clearance Center, Inc.

2.6 Fully Connected Layer

The fully connected layer is used for object classification. It is viewed as the convolutional layer with no weight sharing and reuses the convolutional layer for computation.

$$y = \sum_{m=0}^{M-1} \sum_{n=0}^{N-1} x_{m,n} w_{m,n} \tag{2.6}$$

where

y is the fully connected layer output
x is the fully connected layer input

Exercise

1. Why does the wider and deeper convolutional neural network provide better prediction results?

2. What is the drawback of the wider and deeper neural network?

3. Why is the convolutional layer more critical for deep learning?

4. What is the purpose of the activation layer?

5. What is the drawback of the activation layer?

6. Why is the maximum pooling preferred over the average one?

7. What is BN?

8. What does BN stand for and its function?

9. How is the convolutional layer modified for a fully connected layer?

3

Machine Vision

This chapter describes machine vision and focuses on object recognition. It teaches the machine how to recognize the objects and react differently depending on the object classes. Compared with the traditional computer vision algorithmic approach, it is difficult to cover all features extraction using an algorithmic approach because similar objects may have different features. Deep convolution neural network (DCNN) does not require defining the features for object recognition. DCNN automatically updates the model parameters for feature extraction during the training. It simplifies object recognition and improves overall accuracy. It is easy to target the model for other object recognition through training. This chapter also introduces several machine vision applications, medical diagnosis, retail applications, and airport security.

3.1 Object Recognition

Object recognition [18, 19, 20] (Figures 3.1 and 3.2) is further divided into image classification, object localization, and object detection. The image classification recognizes the objects in the image, then assigns the class labels to the objects. The object localization locates objects in the image and draws a bounding box around the objects. Object detection combines both image classification and object localization. It can detect multiple objects in the image, estimate their size and position, and then draw the bounding box around the objects.

The object detection can also generate the pixel-wise mask over the object to determine the exact object shape and called instance segmentation (Figure 3.3). It can further label each pixel in the image including the background and is called semantic segmentation (Figure 3.4).

Understanding Artificial Intelligence: Fundamentals and Applications, First Edition.
Albert Chun Chen Liu, Oscar Ming Kin Law, and Iain Law.
© 2022 The Institute of Electrical and Electronics Engineers, Inc.
Published 2022 by John Wiley & Sons, Inc.

Image classification   Object localization   Object detection

Figure 3.1 Object recognition examples [19].

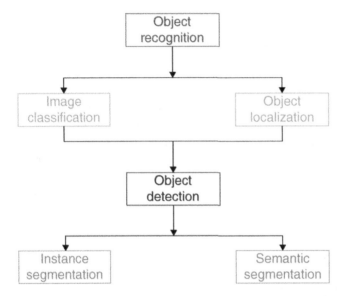

Figure 3.2 Object recognition. Source: Adapted from Sharma [18], Ref. [19], Li et al. [20].

Object detection   Instance segmentation

Figure 3.3 Object detection/instance segmentation [18].

 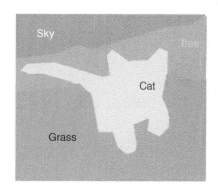

Object detection   Semantic segmentation

Figure 3.4 Object detection/semantic segmentation. Source: Li et al. [20] / Stanford University. / CC0 1.0.

3.2 Feature Matching

Why does object recognition achieve better performance through the convolutional neural network (CNN)? Compared with the traditional computer vision algorithmic approach, CNN does not require defining the object features and performing one-to-one matching. It offers better feature extraction and matching than algorithmic strategies. In the same object class, the features may be varied slightly, and it is difficult to define all the features through programming. For the CNN, the cat and dog's images are convolved with the filter, and it extracts the features (eyes, ears, nose, and mouth) in the image. Then, it filters out the non-existent features through the activation layer and enhances the feature maps using max pooling. The feature maps are fed into the next convolutional layer, and the feature maps (eyes, ears, nose, and mouth) are combined to create the face of the cat and dog. Repeat the same procedure. It goes through the same process (1st, 2nd, 3rd convolution, . . .); it finally creates the cat and dog images (Figure 3.5).

Since the key features (eyes, ears, nose, and mouth) are different between the cat and dog, it can identify the cat and dog in the image. It also explains why a wide and deep CNN is required for object recognition. It combines many small features (wide) and feeds into the multiple convolutional layers (deep) to create complete cat and dog images. The model is not limited to particular cat and dog species. It can be updated through the training with different cat and dog images. Unlike the algorithmic approach, it is required to rewrite the program with additional cat and dog features. It wastes enormous effort for program maintenance.

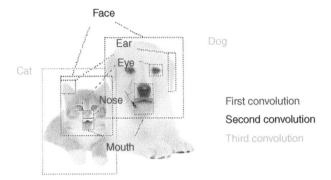

Figure 3.5 Feature extraction/matching [18].

3.3 Facial Recognition

Facial recognition [21, 22] is one of the important object recognition applications. It is used to identify people with facial and emotional expressions (Figures 3.6 and 3.7). This approach is no longer limited to surveillance and security; it is further extended to retail and marketing applications in recent years. It can predict the customer response toward the product through emotional expression, which

Figure 3.6 Facial recognition [21]. Source: Artem/Adobe Stock.

Figure 3.7 Emotion recognition [22]. Source: Stockbusters/Shutterstock.com.

saves enormous time and effort to understand the product demand. By 2022, the facial recognition market is projected about $9.8 billion with a compound annual growth rate (CAGR) of 21.3%.

Facial recognition identifies the people in the images or videos. It is comprised of several major tasks, detection, alignment, extraction, and recognition.

- Facial detection identifies one or more people in the images or videos.
- Facial alignment normalizes the face to be consistent with the facial database.
- Feature extraction extracts the facial features (i.e. eye, ear, nose, and mouth) for the recognition.
- Facial recognition matches the face against known people in the facial database.

With the breakthrough of AlexNet in 2012, multiple neural network models, Deep Face, DeepID, VGGFace, and FaceNet, are proposed between 2014 and 2015. They applied deep learning to simplify facial recognition and achieved 99.15% accuracy, which is better than human accuracy 97.53%. The success of face recognition is widely used for authentication, verification, identification, and emotion detection now.

Affdex emotion software can detect the customer's reaction to the products through 20 facial expressions and seven emotions (anger, contempt, disgust, fear, joy, sadness, and surprise). It can determine the customer's age, gender, ethnic and social status. Based on the detection results, it can understand the product demand, which is important for retail marketing research.

3.4 Gesture Recognition

Gesture recognition [23] (Figure 3.8) in the retail market is expected to grow by 27.54% from 2018 to 2023. The gesture-based interface allows the user to control different devices using hand or body motion. It first captures the hand or body motion through the camera, then analyzes the motion in each frame. Through the machine learning model, it recognizes different motion and identify the gesture, followed by the corresponding actions. It is widely applied to home automation, and people can control home devices through gestures, activate the light, adjust the room temperature, and turn on/off the music system. It can recognize the individual family members and perform the predefined actions based on personal history.

3.5 Machine Vision Applications

This chapter introduces several important machine vision applications in different areas, including medical diagnosis, retail applications, and airport security.

3.5.1 Medical Diagnosis

Medical imaging (ultrasound, X-rays, computerized tomography scan – CT scan, and magnetic resonance imaging – MRI) is a useful cancer diagnosis tool. The doctor spends a significant amount of time examining the medical images

Figure 3.8 Gesture recognition [23]. Source: The Fifth Kingdom/Alamy Stock Photo.

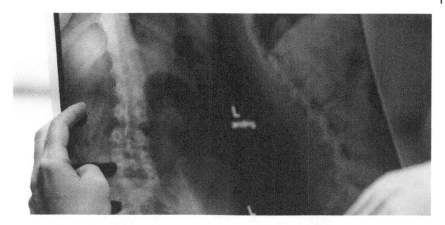

Figure 3.9   Medical diagnosis [24]. Source: Rawpixel.com/Adobe Stock.

and identifying possible cancer. It takes a few hours or days to review all the medical images. Machine vision can quickly detect and identify the subtleties linked with cancer. It filters out the images and highlights the tumor areas in different colors. The doctor only focuses on the filtered images to confirm cancer or not. It saves a lot of time and reduces the doctor's workload. The quick diagnosis offers better treatment in the early cancer stage and increases the chance of survival and cure.

Microsoft offers InnerEye software [24] (Figure 3.9) to identify and highlight the possible tumor in x-ray images visually. The radiologists upload the x-ray images to the system. The software scans through various parts of the organ or ligament in the x-ray image, highlighting the areas with different colors to show possible tumors or other anomalies. The doctor does not waste time examining all the x-ray images and focuses on the InnerEye results. It offers the patient fast and correct treatment.

3.5.2   Retail Applications

Retail also benefits from machine vision, which teaches the machine to recognize the items in the images and videos. It helps the retail to sell the products with better inventory control. Currently, 43% of retail artificial intelligence applications are related to machine vision.

Amazon Go [25] stores utilize the machine vision with "Just Walk Out" technology. Multiple cameras are placed in the aisles and on the shelves (Figure 3.10). It identifies who takes the item from the shelf and links it to the customer's virtual basket. It also removes the item from the virtual basket if the item is returned to the

Figure 3.10 Retail applications. Source: Bishop [25] / GeekWire, LLC.

shelf. The cameras monitor the customers in the store all the time. It sends out the bill to the customers when they walk out of the store. Just Walk Out technology simplifies shopping with better inventory control. The data is directly reported to the sales database. It also notifies the customer when similar items are available. It helps the retail to sell the products with better inventory control and future forecast.

3.5.3 Airport Security

Facial recognition is an important airport security application, especially for passenger processing. It quickly recognizes and validates the passenger's identity and alerts the airport authority for security violations.

Aurora computer services offers Aurora imaging and recognition (AIR) engine [26] (Figure 3.11), which is integrated into the passenger scanning system through software development kit (SDK). The system is trained through the machine learning algorithm with infrared images. It recognizes the facial features from various angles and in different lighting conditions. The system can recognize the passenger's identity, which matches one image to others with facial look-alike and performs the best-match identification. The system alerts the airport authority of the possible passenger and identity mismatch.

Atkins Global has integrated the AIR engine into passenger authentication scanning system (PASS 2) and passed the UK Border Force's security standard for passenger management during Heathrow Airport trials.

Figure 3.11 Airport security [26]. Source: Rawpixel.com/Adobe Stock.

Exercise

1. Why does object recognition achieve better results using CNN?

2. What are three major object recognition techniques?

3. Why is object detection important for machine vision?

4. What is the difference between instance and semantic segmentation?

5. Why is semantic segmentation chosen for autonomous vehicle?

6. How does a CNN recognize different objects in the images?

7. What are the major steps for facial recognition?

8. What are the gesture recognition applications?

9. Why is Amazon Go stores the significant breakthrough in the retail industry?

10. Can you suggest more machine vision applications?

4

Natural Language Processing

The natural language processing (NLP) market [27] (Figure 4.1) grows rapidly in recent years; both the software, hardware, and service markets jump from $5 billion in 2020 to $22.3 billion by 2025 (Figure 4.1). The technology allows the machine to process and understand both spoken and written languages. It also performs complex tasks, machine translation, and dialogue generation. However, NLP faces different levels of ambiguity challenges.

- Word-level ambiguity is related to the word. It is not easy to treat the contraction "won't" as a single word, or two different words, "will not."
- Sentence-level ambiguity is related to the ambiguity of the words in the sentence. "Time flies like an arrow" is a good example; it is difficult to link two different entities, "Time flies" with "an arrow" together. Time is an abstract concept, and an arrow is a real object.
- Meaning-level ambiguity shows the word with several different meanings. There are different meanings for the word "tie." The word "tie" means garment or string (noun). It also means attaching, fastening, or achieving the same goal/ score (verb). It is challenging to define the word "tie" in the sentence.

4.1   Neural Network Model

With artificial intelligence advances, NLP is realized using different neural networks [28, 29]. Unlike traditional algorithmic programming, neural networks do not require predefined features to recognize the language. They are trained by sentence examples for language recognition. Various neural networks are used for

Understanding Artificial Intelligence: Fundamentals and Applications, First Edition.
Albert Chun Chen Liu, Oscar Ming Kin Law, and Iain Law.

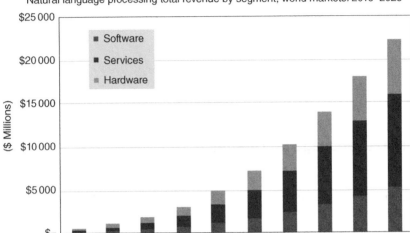

Natural language processing total revenue by segment, world markets: 2016–2025

Figure 4.1 Natural language processing market. Source: Madhavan [27]. Tractica.

different NLP applications, including convolutional neural networks (CNN), recurrent neural networks (RNN), recursive neural networks, and reinforcement learning (RL) models.

4.1.1 Convolutional Neural Network

The CNN is modified for NLP (Figure 4.2). The sentence is first tokenized into the words, then transformed into a word embedding matrix through the look-up table. It convolves the matrix with the filter to create the feature maps and feeds into the max pooling, followed by the fully connected layer to generate the sentence representation. The CNN is targeted for word-based prediction and other language tasks, such as name entity recognition (NER), part of speech (POS), and aspect detection. It works with the window-based approach, where each word is related to the fixed-size window of neighboring words. It is further enhanced through dynamic convolutional neural network (DCNN) with a dynamic k-max-pooling strategy to support the variable word range.

The CNN is used not only for sentence modeling but also for aspect detection, sentiment analysis, short text categorization, and sarcasm detection.

4.1.2 Recurrent Neural Network

The RNN is useful to process the context-dependent human language (Figure 4.3) because the words are related to each other in the sentence. It performs the computation on current data as well as the previous results and applies the

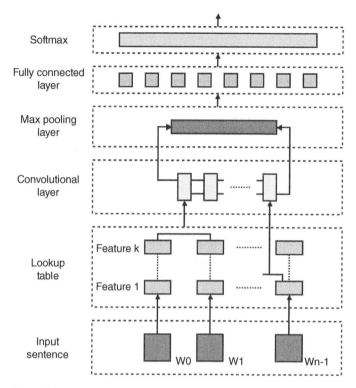

Figure 4.2 Convolutional neural network. Source: Adapted from Elvis [28].

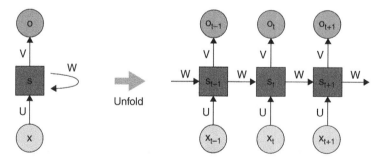

Figure 4.3 Recurrent neural network. Source: Adapted from Elvis [28].

sequence-to-sequence (seq2seq) model for language translation. It is quite suitable for word-level classification, sentence-level classification, semantic match, machine translation, and image caption.

$$s_t = f\left(Ux_t + Ws_{t-1}\right) \tag{4.1}$$

$$o_t = f\left(Vs_t\right) \tag{4.2}$$

The drawback of the RNN is the vanishing gradient issue. If the neural network weights are small, the subsequent weights become smaller and close to zero. It results in slow training and prediction errors. Therefore, long short-term memory (LSTM) is proposed to solve this problem.

4.1.2.1 Long Short-Term Memory Network

The LSTM [30] (Figure 4.4) is modified from the RNN with multiple gates, input gate, forget gate, and output gate.

- Input gate controls the input data transferred to the memory.
- Forget gate controls the stored data for computation.
- Output gate controls the output data for prediction.

The LSTM network introduces the additional gates that preserve and forget the data. It controls the data fed into the network for operation and computes the hidden state value through the combination of three gates resulting in the following equations. It eliminates the data-dependent issue and resolves the gradient vanishing problem.

$$f_t = \sigma\left(W_f\left[h_t \cdot x_t\right] + b_f\right) \tag{4.3}$$

$$i_t = \sigma\left(W_i\left[h_t \cdot x_t\right] + b_i\right) \tag{4.4}$$

$$c_t' = \tanh\left(W_C\left[h_t \cdot x_t\right] + b_C\right) \tag{4.5}$$

$$c_t = f_t \otimes c_{t-1} + i_t \otimes c_t' \tag{4.6}$$

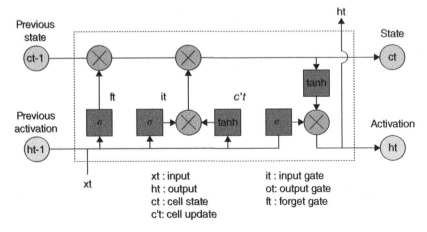

Figure 4.4 Long short-term memory network. Source: Adapted from Elvis [28].

$$o_t = \sigma\left(W_o\left[h_t \cdot x_t\right] + b_o\right) \tag{4.7}$$

$$h_t = o_t \otimes \tanh\left(c_t\right) \tag{4.8}$$

The LSTM network is suitable for machine translation, text summarization, human conversations, and question answers tasks.

4.1.3 Recursive Neural Network

Recursive neural network (Figure 4.5) is used to model the human language where the words and sub-phrases composed the higher-level phrase in a hierarchical structure. The words are stored in the child nodes and grouped to form the sub-phrases; the sub-phrases are regrouped recursively to create the final sentence representation.

The recursive neural networks are applied for parsing, sentimental analysis, and sentence relatedness.

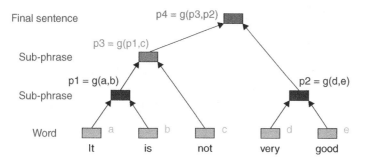

Figure 4.5 Recursive neural network.

4.1.4 Reinforcement Learning

The RL (Figure 4.6) is useful for dialogue generation. It applies the RNN-based generative model (agent) to respond to the input word (external environment) and predicts the next word of the sentence (action) to maximize the reward. It also updates the model's internal states every cycle. The process is continued until the end of the sentence for the dialogue generation.

It is required to handle the states and actions properly to ensure correct prediction, then adversarial training is used. It trains the generator to create the machine word sequence and makes the discriminator not distinguish between the machine and human word sequence, then achieves the accurate prediction.

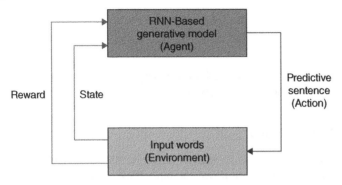

Figure 4.6 Reinforcement learning. Source: Adapted from Elvis [28].

4.2 Natural Language Processing Applications

This chapter lists several interesting NLP applications, virtual assistant, language translation, and machine transcription.

4.2.1 Virtual Assistant

Virtual assistants [31, 32] (Figure 4.7) (i.e. Google Home and Amazon Alexa) are widely used in everyday life, which control the home devices (light bulbs, power outlets, and thermostat), access the public information (news, weather, bus

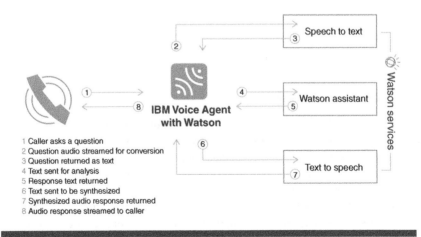

Figure 4.7 IBM Watson assistant. Source: de Jesus [31].

schedule, an upcoming event), and enjoy the entertainment (music, movie, video). Amazon Alexa [33] offers an additional programming capability, Alexa skill kit (ASK), which is a software development platform. It allows the users to create their interactive voice applications (called skills) to perform everyday tasks. Over 30 000 skills are developed to control different devices. Amazon also promotes the "Alexa Everywhere" strategy. It works with Google, Apple, Microsoft, and other companies to develop products that are designed to watch you, listen to you, and follow you around.

Virtual assistants also support multiple business applications, such as healthcare, finance, and retail. United Bank of Switzerland AG (UBS) works with IBM to offer virtual financial assistant for the customers. The assistant fully utilizes the speech-to-text and text-to-speech technology. It first converts the customers' conversation into the text and searches the corresponding answers in the database, then converts it back to speech and answers the customers' questions.

UBS offers two virtual financial assistants, Fin and Daniel. Fin is used to manage simple tasks, answer simple inquiries, and replace/cancel credit cards. Daniel is developed for professional financial management, which helps the customers to manage the investment. It answers the investment questions and provides the stock market guideline based on the historical data.

4.2.2 Language Translation

With artificial intelligence advances, the language translation [34, 35] (Figure 4.8) achieves higher accuracy through the neural machine translation (NMT) (Figure 4.8). The translator is trained through many translated sentences, and the translation is based on the sentence's context rather than the grammatical rules and bilingual dictionary. Many business translators are further customized to

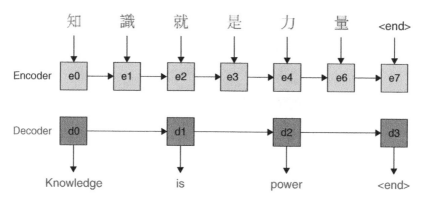

Figure 4.8 Google translate. Source: Madhavan [34].

handle professional terminology (healthcare, finance, legal) through training data because the normal translator cannot translate the professional terms correctly.

Currently, Google Translate is the most significant player in business-to-consumer (B2C) translation. It employs the Google neural machine translation (GNMT) system, which considers the input sentence as a single unit for translation rather than breaking it into the individual word. For Chinese to English translation, it encodes the Chinese words as a list of vectors, and each vector represents the meaning of the words (Encoder). After the whole sentence is read, it decodes the sentence and generates the English phrase.

4.2.3 Machine Transcription

Machine transcription [36, 37] plays an important role in artificial intelligence applications (Figure 4.9), which analyze a large amount of data (text and speech) for prediction. Machine transcription needs to overcome multiple challenges, different voices, various languages, heavy accents, and background noise.

The healthcare industry shows a growing interest in machine transcription because doctors spend 49% of work hours to complete administrative tasks, especially for electronic health record (EHR). Machine transcription can automate the clinical documenting process. It captures the medical terminology and integrates it into the EHR system, which includes the note into the patient records for future treatment. Robin Healthcare offers the software Robin, which is integrated with the smart speakers in the clinic. When the doctors communicate with the patients, the speakers automatically record the conversation and transcribe it into the text without any wake words and particular diction. It also nicely formats the transcript and transfer it into the patient records in the EHR system.

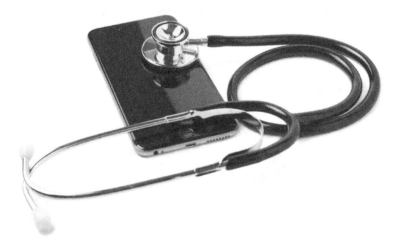

Figure 4.9 Medical transcription [36]. Source: Dmitri Stalnuhhin/Adobe Stock.

Exercise

1. What are the major challenges of NLP?

2. How is the CNN modified for NLP?

3. Why is the RNN important for NLP?

4. How does an LSTM network solve RNN problems?

5. How does the recursive neural network handle NLP?

6. Why is RL useful for dialogue generation?

7. How does the virtual assistant support the customers in banking?

8. How does Google Translate perform the language translation?

9. How does medical transcription reduce the doctor's workload?

10. Can you suggest more NLP applications?

5

Autonomous Vehicle

After several years of development, the autonomous vehicle [38, 39] (Figure 5.1) becomes mature. Automotive manufacturers release different levels of autonomous vehicles. By estimation, the global autonomous vehicle market is increased from \$54.23 billion in 2019 to \$556.67 billion by 2026, with an annual growth rate of 39.47%. The autonomous vehicle's success depends on the breakthrough of artificial intelligence, machine vision, and the maturity of the internet of things (IoT). This chapter introduces basic autonomous vehicle technology, communication strategies, law legislation, and future challenges.

5.1 Levels of Driving Automation

According to the society of automotive engineers (SAE) International, the autonomous vehicle is divided into five levels of automation [40, 41] (Figure 5.2):

- Level 0 (No Automation) – The driver manually controls the vehicle and performs all the driving tasks, including steering, acceleration, braking, etc.
- Level 1 (Driving Assistance) – The vehicle offers the essential features to support driving. The adaptive cruise control (ACC) controls the engine and brake for speed variation. It still requires the driver to control the driving all the time.
- Level 2 (Partial Automation) – Advanced driver assistance (ADA) performs the acceleration, braking, and steering. It requires the driver to monitor the driving and take control at any time.
- Level 3 (Conditional Automation) – The vehicle can perform most of the driving tasks under specific conditions. It requires the driver to override the driving for environmental changes.

Understanding Artificial Intelligence: Fundamentals and Applications, First Edition.
Albert Chun Chen Liu, Oscar Ming Kin Law, and Iain Law.
© 2022 The Institute of Electrical and Electronics Engineers, Inc.
Published 2022 by John Wiley & Sons, Inc.

Figure 5.1 Autonomous vehicle [39]. Source: Metamorworks/Adobe Stock.

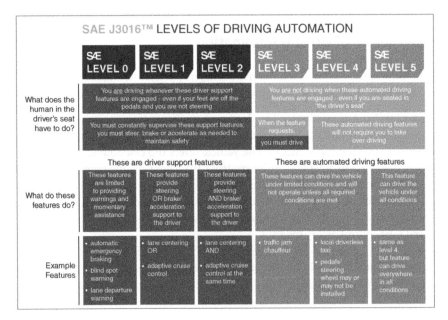

Figure 5.2 Levels of driving automation. Source: Stayton and Stilgoe [40] / with permission of SAE International.

- Level 4 (High Automation) – The vehicle performs all the driving tasks safely under specific circumstances with geofencing. It is an option for the driver to override the driving tasks.
- Level 5 (Full Automation) – The vehicle performs all the driving tasks without the driver's interaction.

5.2 Autonomous Technology

The autonomous vehicle [42, 43, 44] employs various technologies to support driving automation, including computer vision, sensor fusion, localization, path planning, and driving control (Figure 5.3).

5.2.1 Computer Vision

Computer vision [45] (Figure 5.4) is the key feature of the autonomous vehicle. It can detect static and moving objects, such as pedestrians, cyclists, vehicles, traffic lights, and road signs, through a 360-degree view of its surroundings. After the camera captures those images, they are fed into the machine learning algorithm to identify the objects and determine the corresponding actions. For example, if the vehicle detects the traffic light switched from green to yellow, it slows down the vehicle and stops before the traffic light. If the child suddenly crosses the street, it immediately applies the brake to avoid a collision.

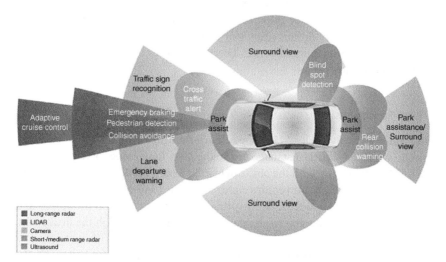

Figure 5.3 Autonomous technology. Source: Bayyou [43] / International Journal of Emerging Technology in Computer Science and Electronics.

Figure 5.4 Computer vision technology [45]. Source: Image courtesy of NVIDIA.

The autonomous vehicle not only applies computer vision for object detection but also employs audio recognition technology. It recognizes emergency vehicles' sounds (ambulance, police car, fire truck) and makes way for those vehicles. With computer vision and audio recognition, it assists the driver in performing the driving tasks. The drawback of those technologies is poor accuracy and precision under bad weather conditions (rain, storm, fog, and snow). It is difficult to identify the objects during thunderstorms. Therefore, sensor fusion is used to enhance autonomous vehicle safety.

5.2.2 Sensor Fusion

Most autonomous vehicles [45] are equipped with ultrasound sensors to detect objects within a short distance and radar for long-range object detection (Figure 5.5). It links up with the object detection results for distance measurement (Table 5.1). Tesla vehicle [46] equips eight cameras for 360-degree view with 250 m measuring range. It applies the twelve ultrasound sensors to detect the objects and employs the additional radar to enable the vehicle to see through the heavy rain, fog, dust, and the car ahead.

The light detection and ranging (LIDAR) technology further enhances distance measurement, which applies a pulsed laser to measure the distance and

Figure 5.5 Radar technology [45]. Source: Metawave.

Table 5.1 Sensor technology comparison.

	Ultrasound	Radar	Lidar
Cost	Low	Medium	High
Size	Small	Small/Medium	Medium/Large
Detection speed	Low	High	Medium
Color sensitivity	No	No	No
Weather robustness	High	High	Medium
Day/night support	High	High	High
Resolution	Low	Medium	High
Range	Short	Short/Medium/Long	Long

creates an accurate 3D view of the surrounding objects. However, the poor weather can scatter laser light resulting in a false reading. A new technology, Hemera, overcomes the limitation; it successfully detects the objects 54 m away. LIDAR scanner is relatively large and expensive and has not been adopted by all autonomous vehicles yet.

5.2.3 Localization

The autonomous vehicle [47] can see and listen. It is also important to know where you are. The localization is realized through a global positioning system (GPS) with detailed maps (Figure 5.6). It shows the exact location and intersections, which provides the drivers with a complete list of points of interest (shops, restaurants, gas stations, schools, and parks). The drivers know where they are going. They can plan the trip and calculate the travel times.

Moreover, the autonomous vehicle also receives additional traffic information through vehicle-to-vehicle (V2V) and vehicle-to-infrastructure (V2I) communication.[1] It allows the autonomous vehicle to alter the route to avoid traffic congestion and car accident. With the support of computer vision and sensor technology, it calibrates the vehicle position through the distance measurement between the surrounding landmarks. It increases the position accuracy from +/–3 m (GPS) to +/–10 cm (LIDAR). As a result, the autonomous vehicle can safely arrive at the destination without human intervention.

5.2.4 Path Planning

Path planning [48] is used to replicate human driving thinking and decision (Figure 5.7). It reads the map, analyzes the surrounding environment, and decides the optimal actions based on speed, road conditions, traffic rules, and safety.

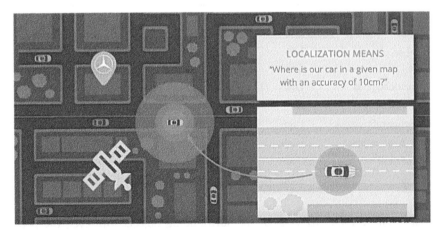

Figure 5.6 Localization technology [47]. Source: These images reproduced with permission from Udacity, Inc.

---

1 Please refer to Section 5.3 communication strategies.

Figure 5.7 Path planning technology [48]. Source: These images reproduced with permission from Udacity, Inc.

Computer vision and sensor fusion construct precise pictures of the surrounding objects' position and speed. It predicts the trajectories of surrounding objects to avoid a collision. It also determines the driving behavior and makes the final driving decision. When the autonomous vehicle passes the slow-moving vehicle, it first determines the slow-moving vehicle speed and the adjacent lane moving vehicles, then decides to switch to the left or the right lane to bypass the vehicle. It may cancel the bypass action due to traffic condition changes.

5.2.5 Drive Control

Every year, 1.35 million people are killed in traffic accidents in the world. It is estimated almost 3700 death every day. Most of the accidents are caused by human errors and result in over $600 billion loss from death and injuries. The autonomous vehicle offers a fast response and makes the correct decision (steering, acceleration, and braking) through Automatic Driver Assistance (ADA) to avoid traffic accidents. If the vehicle travels at the speed of 65 mph (100 km/h), it has traveled a distance of 48 ft (13 m) with 0.5 second reaction time. The fast response time can avoid fatal accidents and save the life. Tesla [49] has offered Traffic-Aware Cruise Control (Figure 5.8) to maintain the driving speed and autosteer to travel within the marked lane. It also performs the auto lane change to switch between the lanes. Enhanced autopilot guides the car from a highway's on-ramp to off-ramp,

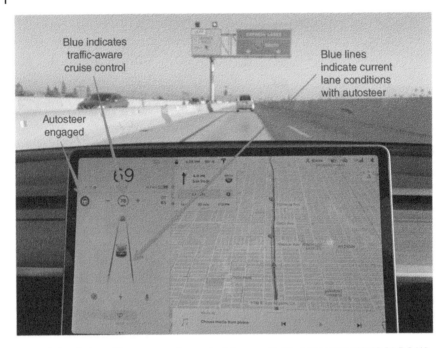

Figure 5.8 Tesla traffic-aware cruise control. Source: Podfeet [49] / CC BY-NC-SA 3.0 US.

including suggesting lane changes, navigating interchanges, automatically engaging the turn signal, and taking the correct exit. When the autosteer is engaged, it assists the car to move to an adjacent lane on the highway. It also identifies the traffic lights and stop signs, which slows the car and stops automatically in the city.

5.3 Communication Strategies

Besides the driving automation technologies, autonomous vehicles also communicate with other vehicles and surroundings to improve efficiency and safety. The communication strategies [39] are divided into V2V, V2I, and vehicle-to-pedestrian (V2P) interaction.

5.3.1 Vehicle-to-Vehicle Communication

V2V communication [50] (Figure 5.9) allows the driving information (speed, location, direction, braking) and traffic conditions (congestion, hazard, obstacle) to exchange between the vehicles through the dedicated short-range radio communication (DSRC). The vehicle can activate other vehicles' automatic emergency braking (AEB) to avoid the potential collision during the emergency braking or sudden lane change. When the

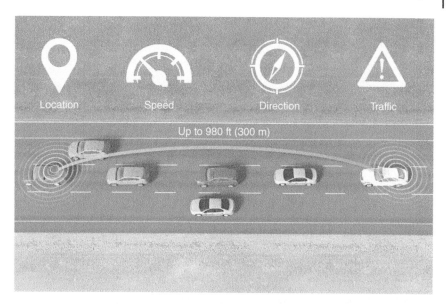

Figure 5.9 Vehicle-to-vehicle communication. Source: Koon [50] / ENGINEERING.com.

vehicle encounters traffic congestion due to car accidents, it relays the information to other vehicles to alternate the route to avoid traffic delays.

5.3.2   Vehicle-to-Infrastructure Communication

V2I communication [51] (Figure 5.10) allows the vehicle to communicate with the Intelligent Transport System (road camera, street sensor, traffic light, and parking meter) to capture real-time road conditions. It detects the number of vehicles on the road during rush hours and dynamically adjusts the traffic light time interval to reduce the vehicle waiting time. It not only improves the road conditions but also avoids traffic congestion. The vehicle can communicate with the parking garage to locate the space for route planning. It can also reserve the parking space before the journey to save travel time. This approach is important for smart city development, which reduces the number of cars driving around looking for a parking space.

5.3.3   Vehicle-to-Pedestrian Communication

V2P communication [52] (Figure 5.11) allows the vehicle to interact with the pedestrian smartphone. It alerts the vehicle about the pedestrian position and avoids collision. When the pedestrian steps into the crosswalk, it activates the crosswalk signal to alert the driver, especially in bad weather conditions (rain, fog, and snow). It helps to prevent pedestrian injuries and deaths.

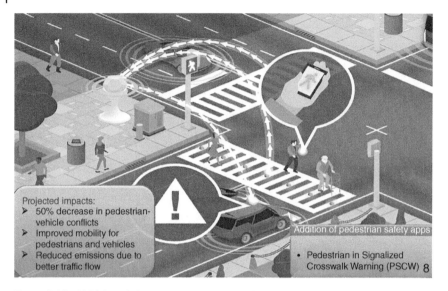

Figure 5.10 Vehicle to infrastructure communication. Source: Ref. [51].

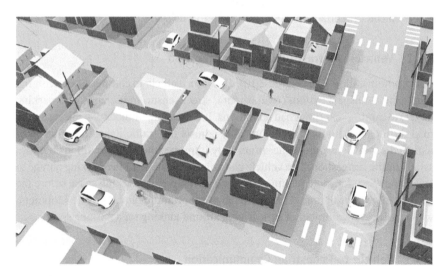

Figure 5.11 Vehicle-to-pedestrian communication. Source: Ref. [52].

5.4   Law Legislation

In the United States, the federal, state, and local governments have already introduced legislation for autonomous vehicle testing and deployment [53, 54] (Figure 5.12), which covers several different areas:

- Perception and response
- System safety and reliability
- Vehicle cybersecurity
- Privacy
- Human–machine interface
- Crashworthiness
- Post-crash behavior
- Ethical consideration

5.4.1   Human Behavior

Human behavior [53] is one of the important factors of car accidents. Level 2 and level 3 automation can perform over 90% of driving tasks and becomes safer to

Figure 5.12   Autonomous vehicle law legislation. Source: zapp2photo/Adobe Stock.

avoid car accidents. However, the autonomous vehicle driver is easily distracted, resulting in catastrophic failure. In May 2016, a serious accident happened, Tesla (autopilot mode) collided with a tractor-trailer. The trailer was visible to the Tesla driver for at least 7 seconds before the collision, but the driver did not pay any attention to avoid it. It is not only for the manufacturer to offer the system to keep the driver alert, but the driver is also responsible for the driving safety.

5.4.2 Lability

Currently, people are concerned about legal liability issues. Suppose the vehicle involves an accident with level 2 or 3 of automation, who is responsible for the loss, the automotive manufacturers, or the software developers. Currently, Mercedes, Volvo, Waymo (Google) accept the liability for hardware and software failure. It is still difficult to determine the legal liability. If the autonomous vehicle has warned the driver, the driver does not take any action in time. Is the driver of the vehicle at fault? The lawmakers continue to explore how to legislate autonomous vehicles. Until the legislation is finalized, the driver must put the hands on the steering wheel for level 2 or 3 autonomous vehicles and respond to any emergency conditions. In the United States, liability insurance is set between \$2 and \$5 million for autonomous vehicle testing and provides basic protection for other drivers and pedestrians.

5.4.3 Regulation

In the United States, the government supports autonomous vehicle development, but they do not have the complete regulations to make it work. Congress works with the Department of Transportation to set up the national rules for autonomous vehicles; however, 20 states have developed their own rules, and three states offer executive orders to help the manufacturers to test the autonomous vehicles and deploy them for commercial use. Moreover, the political opposition is emerged to slow or stop the legislation due to the direct competition (i.e. taxi and truck drivers).

In China, the government applies another approach, which redesigns the urban landscapes, infrastructure, and policies to support an autonomous vehicle driving-friendly environment. The legislation is not limited to the vehicle but also the pedestrian. It significantly speeds up autonomous vehicle deployment.

5.5 Future Challenges

Autonomous vehicles are currently in testing in the United States. They still face numerous challenges [39] soon.

5.5.1 Road Rules Variation

Since the road rules are varied from country to country under different traffic conditions, it is difficult for the autonomous system to support all the road rules, especially for developing countries. The developer should consider migrating the autonomous systems to other countries to handle the unique traffic conditions. The new set of traffic data must be fed into the machine learning algorithm for training. Since the driving responses vary widely across countries, it takes time to migrate the system to different countries.

5.5.2 Unified Communication Protocol

To execute different vehicle communication strategies, the unified communication protocol must be well defined. It allows the traffic information to exchange among the vehicle, infrastructure, and pedestrians. Besides the technical challenges, it should also consider cybersecurity and protect personal privacy. The unified communication protocol is not limited to one country only, which must be recognized and supported globally. The international committee should be established to define the communication strategies for autonomous vehicles.

5.5.3 Safety Standard and Guidelines

The autonomous vehicle is a new technology without records. It is not easy to define the standard and guidelines to fulfill all the requirements. The government should first define a set of safety standards and guidelines for different kinds of vehicles; then, it collects the feedback and considers new development to revise the standards and guidelines within a period. The safety standards and guidelines are subject to change for a higher level of automation.

5.5.4 Weather/Disaster

How does the autonomous vehicle handle bad weather and natural disaster (thunderstorms, snowstorms, freezing rain, flooding, and mudslide)? The developer must simulate the autonomous vehicles under bad weather and define different responses to handle an emergency. Additional information must be provided to the driver to control the autonomous vehicle under severe weather conditions manually. It is the biggest challenge for autonomous vehicle development.

Exercise

1. What are the five levels of automation for the autonomous vehicle?

2. What are the key features of the autonomous vehicle?

3. How do we improve the safety through driver monitoring and path planning?

4. What are the major challenges for V2V communication?

5. How can the government support V2I development?

6. Why is V2P communication important?

7. What are the major issues related to autonomous vehicle legislation?

8. What are the road rules difference between the United States and developing countries?

9. How do you suggest more safety standards/guidelines for the autonomous vehicle?

10. How can the autonomous vehicle handle severe weather conditions?

6

Drone

A drone, also called the unmanned aerial vehicle (UAV), becomes affordable for hobbyists in recent years, and it is widely applied for aerial photography and filming. The hobbyist takes aerial photos/videos using the flying drone, especially for the first-person view (FPV). It lets the photographers see the world from a bird's eye view through google. With artificial intelligence success, the drone is no longer limited to recreational use. It is also used for commercial applications, civil construction, agriculture, and emergency rescue.

6.1 Drone Design

There are two major drone designs [55], the fixed-wing and rotary-wing drones (Figure 6.1). The fixed-wing drone is used for long-distance flights at high speed. When the fixed-wing drone moves forward, the air passes through the wing to create the lift force and allows the drone to stay in the air. It is more efficient than the rotary-wing drone. However, the trained pilot must operate the fixed-wing drone with a long runway for take-off and landing. It is not so popular among hobbyists.

The rotary-wing drone is easy to operate and hover in the air for photography and filming. The typical travel distance is limited to two miles with less than 30 minutes of flight time. Due to the cost and operation, the rotary-wing drone is more attractive for hobbyists.

6.2 Drone Structure

Currently, the drone employs various flight technologies [56], including the camera, gyro stabilization, a global positioning system (GPS), collision avoidance, and sensors (Figure 6.2).

Understanding Artificial Intelligence: Fundamentals and Applications, First Edition.
Albert Chun Chen Liu, Oscar Ming Kin Law, and Iain Law.
© 2022 The Institute of Electrical and Electronics Engineers, Inc.
Published 2022 by John Wiley & Sons, Inc.

Design	Fixed wing drone	Rotary wing drone
Cruise speed	High	Low
Area coverage	Large	Small
Flight times	Long	Short
Take-off/Landing	Large	Small
Wind resistance	High	Low

Figure 6.1 Unmanned aerial vehicle design. Source: Adapted from Ref. [55].

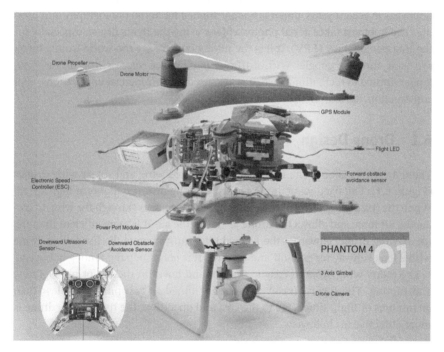

Figure 6.2 Drone structure. Source: French [56] / TECHMAG.

6.2.1   Camera

The camera is the key feature of the drone. It captures the 360-degree aerial view at a low cost. The video camera resolution is recently increased to 4k, which offers the best picture quality for photography and filming.

Additional gimbals are used to stabilize the camera with an inertial measurement unit (IMU). It responds to the drone motion and sends feedback to the controller to keep the camera stable on each axis. It avoids the camera shake, and the photos are out of focus or blurry. It is further divided into two-axis and three-axis gimbals. The two-axis gimbals stabilize in the pitch and roll axis. The three-axis one stabilizes the camera on all three-axis.

6.2.2   Gyro Stabilization

Gyro stabilization is developed for stabilizing the flight; the gyroscope senses the drone orientation and adjusts the flight to counteract the rotation; it offers six-axis gyro stabilization based on the six degrees of freedom, including the x-axis, y-axis, z-axis, lateral axis (pitch), the longitudinal axis (roll), and the vertical axis (yaw) (Figure 6.3).

Gyro stabilization is important for the drone to stay steady in a windy environment and capture aerial photos.

6.2.3   Collision Avoidance

Since the drone flies at high speed, the pilot may not respond to the obstacle that quickly resulted in the crash. The drone applies ultrasound or infrared sensors to measure the surrounding object's distance through the time of flight. It sends the

Figure 6.3   Six degree of freedom.

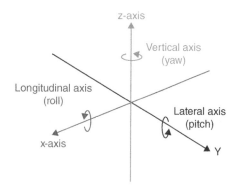

measurement results back to the controller to maneuver around the obstacles (i.e. walls, trees, rocks, and buildings). The collision avoidance automatically avoids the obstacles without being manually piloted. It is the standard feature for the advanced drone design.

6.2.4 Global Positioning System

The drone offers an additional GPS to record the flight position and stores the geolocation in photos and videos. The geotagged photos and videos are important for commercial applications, agriculture, land surveying, and emergency rescue. Moreover, most of the drone employs the "Return to Home" feature, which records the take-off zone (home) position and lets the drone automatically returns to the home.

6.2.5 Sensors

The drone employs additional sensors to determine the drone position and orientation

- The accelerometer measures the attitude to perform the flight correction.
- The magnetometer measures the magnetic force to act as the compass to identify the flight direction.
- The barometer measures the attitude through the air pressure changes.
- The tilt sensor measures the drone motion and combines with the accelerometer and gyroscope to stabilize the flight.
- The current sensor monitors the electrical current flow to optimize the battery usage and detects any electrical failure.

6.3 Drone Regulation

In the United States, all drones must be registered with Federal Aviation Administration (FAA), except for the weight of less than 0.55 lbs (250 g). In 2021, an additional remote ID is required for the drones to operate. The remote ID provides the drone identity, location, altitude, control station, and take-off location. The drones are subjected to the rules issued by the FAA[1], which enables the safe operation of the drone and avoids the drone flying in restricted airspace. The rules are further divided into recreational and commercial use.

---

1 Please refer to Federal Aviation Administration (FAA) website: https://www.faa.gov for latest drone regulations.

6.3.1 Recreational Rules

- Register your drone, mark it on the outside with the registration number and carry proof of registration.
- Fly only for recreational purposes.
- Fly your drone at or below 400 ft above the ground when in uncontrolled airspace.
- Keep your drone within your visual line of sight or within the visual line-of-sight of a visual observer who is co-located (physically next to) and in direct communication with you.
- Do not fly at night unless your drone has lighting that allows you to know its location and orientation at all times.
- Give way to and do not interfere with manned aircraft.
- Never fly over any person or moving vehicle.
- Never interfere with emergency response activities such as disaster relief, any type of accident response, law enforcement activities, firefighting, or hurricane recovery efforts.
- Never fly under the influence of drugs or alcohol. Many over-the-counter medications have side effects that could impact your ability to operate your drone safely.
- Do not operate your drone carelessly or recklessly.

6.3.2 Commercial Rules

- Always avoid manned aircraft.
- Never operate carelessly or recklessly.
- Keep your drone within sight. If you use First Person View or similar technology, you must have a visual observer always keep your drone within unaided sight (for example, no binoculars).
- You cannot be a pilot or visual observer for more than one drone operation at a time.
- Do not fly a drone over people unless they are directly participating in the operation.
- Do not operate your drone from a moving vehicle or aircraft unless flying your drone over a sparsely populated area. It does not involve the transportation of property for compensation or hires.
- You can fly during daylight (30 minutes before official sunrise to 30 minutes after official sunset, local time) or in twilight if your drone has anti-collision lighting.
- Minimum weather visibility is three miles from your control station.
- The maximum allowable altitude is 400 ft above the ground, higher if your drone remains within 400 ft of a structure.
- The maximum speed is 100 mph (87 knots).

6.4 Applications

This chapter describes several popular commercial drone applications, civil construction, agriculture, and emergency rescue.

6.4.1 Infrastructure Inspection

Drone [57] also provides cheaper, faster, and safer ways for infrastructure inspection and maintenance (Figure 6.4). The New York Authority applies the drone to inspect the ice boom near Lake Erie; it only costs $300, which is less than the helicopter ($3500) and the boat ($3300) expense. Several energy companies (i.e. Southern Company and Duke Energy) deploy drones to inspect the power plants, power lines, and storm damages (Figure 6.4).

6.4.2 Civil Construction

Drone [58] performs real-time aerial inspection for the construction site (Figure 6.5). It can quickly survey the site and identify potential problems. It detects the area strained by weather damage or leaks through the thermal camera. With the aerial images, the engineer can prioritize the issues and make the correct decision to solve the problems. The drone also replaces the labor in a dangerous environment and identifies the hazards on the construction site. After the drones are used, the construction accidents are reduced by 90%.

The drone is also used to create 3D models or maps in construction. It captures a large number of high-resolution photos. The images are overlapped that same point in the images is visible in multiple photos from different vantage points. It applies the machine learning algorithm to create the 3D models or maps from

Figure 6.4 Infrastructure inspection and maintenance [57]. Source: JEAN PIERRE MULLER/AFP/Getty Images.

Figure 6.5 Civil construction [58]. Source: Kadmy/Adobe Stock.

those vantage points with different depth perceptions. Finally, it can print out the models and maps using a 3D printer.

6.4.3 Agriculture

With artificial intelligence success, the drone [59] is widely used for planting, spraying, irrigation, monitoring, soil and field analysis, and crop health assessment (Figure 6.6). Sensefly offers a computer vision drone, which captures infrared images of the field to monitor crop growth and access soil conditions. The software plans the flight path and covers the whole area. During the flight, the drone uploads the aerial images into the cloud server. The machine learning algorithm searches the database and then recognizes the plant and soil conditions, including the temperature, moisture, and soil conditions. The drone can cover 200 hectares (500 acres) per flight and 500 ft (120 m) above the ground. It helps the farmers to improve crop growth at a low cost.

6.4.4 Emergency Rescue

The drone [60] provides many benefits for emergency rescue (Figure 6.7). It can operate in a dangerous environment and outperform humans. The drone helps to search the missing people and rescues the injuries. Compared with the rescue helicopter, the basic cost of a helicopter is over $1.5 M, and the operating cost is about $1500 per hour; the cost of a drone is less than $3000, and the operating cost

Figure 6.6 Agricultural drone [59]. Source: kinwun/Adobe Stock.

Figure 6.7 Search and rescue drone [60]. Source: pixone3d / Adobe stock.

is under $100. The drone is a cost-effective solution and provides a quick response to save numerous lives.

Moreover, the drone maps the natural damages (wildfire, flooding, and earthquake) to a 3D landscape model, which provides a clear view of the disastrous damage. It gives a better insight to rebuild the disastrous areas and prioritize the reconstruction after the catastrophe.

Exercise

1. What are the major differences between fixed-wing and rotary-wing drones?

2. What are the key drone technologies?

3. What are the recreational rules of the drone?

4. What are the commercial rules of the drone?

5. What are the future drone development directions?

6. How do drones apply for infrastructure inspection?

7. How do drones apply for civil construction?

8. How does the drone play an important role in agriculture?

9. Why is the drone a cost-effective solution for emergency rescue?

10. Can you suggest several drone applications?

7

Healthcare

In the United States, it spends much more on healthcare than other countries, however, over 32.8 million Americans have no health insurance, and 58 million Americans cannot afford prescription medicines. Pharmaceutical companies often overcharge prescription medicines. They raise the price of drugs due to the huge research and development cost, high marketing spending, and good profit margin. It results in serious medication affordability problems.

Moreover, the doctors spend an enormous amount of time on administrative paperwork, especially for electronic health record (EHR), and pay less attention to the patients. It causes a doctor shortage and leads to high healthcare costs. Artificial intelligence [61–64] has started to transform the healthcare system and solve long-lasting problems. It improves drug development, speeds up the medical diagnosis, performs the radiological analysis, monitors the health conditions, and simplifies the administrative paperwork. It significantly reduces the overall healthcare expenses.

7.1 Telemedicine

If the patients live in rural areas, they are geographically isolated from the healthcare facilities (clinic, laboratory, hospital). They spend a lot of time traveling long distances to visit the nearest healthcare facilities. They may not get the medical screening examination for early disease detection and miss the chance to receive treatment with more prolonged survival. Artificial intelligence [65] can solve problems and improve the quality of life.

During the pandemic period, telemedicine (Figure 7.1) becomes the alternative for clinic visits. The doctor examines the patients through telephone and video

Understanding Artificial Intelligence: Fundamentals and Applications, First Edition.
Albert Chun Chen Liu, Oscar Ming Kin Law, and Iain Law.
© 2022 The Institute of Electrical and Electronics Engineers, Inc.
Published 2022 by John Wiley & Sons, Inc.

Figure 7.1 Telehealth/telemedicine. Source: Faggella [65] / Emerj Artificial Intelligence Research.

conference. The patient can obtain the basic vital information (temperature, blood pressure, heart rate, and echocardiogram) through smart medical devices (smartwatch or wristband), then transfer the information to the doctor electronically. It avoids the long travel time for healthcare facilities visits. With artificial intelligence support, a large amount of vital information is analyzed through a machine learning algorithm. If the medical device detects abnormal blood pressure or irregular heartbeats, it evaluates the risk of stroke or heart attack and alerts the patient for early treatment immediately. Telemedicine is continued to evolve, and patients can receive the best medical treatment regardless of geographical restrictions in the near future.

7.2 Medical Diagnosis

Medical errors are the third-highest cause of death in the United States. The doctor needs to examine the patient with enormous vital signs and makes the correct diagnosis within a short period. A small mistake may lead to serious medical errors. Artificial intelligence [66–68] can help doctors to prevent medical errors (Figure 7.2). It collects thousands of vital signs and symptoms of the diseases, then analyzes the information to identify the health issue with diagnosis advice. It also recommends additional medical screening tests (blood tests and X-rays) for further examination and helps the doctor make the correct diagnosis. Moreover, it can alert the doctor about the patent's risk factors to provide the patient with the best personal care management. Machine learning can continue to learn the symptoms of different diseases to improve diagnosis accuracy. It not only

Figure 7.2 Medical diagnosis [66]. Source: Sergey Nivens / Adobe Stock.

avoids medical errors with correct diagnosis and treatment. The patient can receive the treatment in an early stage to reduce the treatment cost and speed up the recovery process.

7.3 Medical Imaging

Artificial intelligence [69, 70] can be applied for computer-aided cancer detection, 3D image processing organ auto-segmentation, and machine learning imaging analysis (Figure 7.3). It is not widely used yet because most doctors do not fully understand the importance of artificial intelligence, which can accurately analyze and interpret medical imaging.

Artificial intelligence applies object recognition for cancer detection through medical imaging (mammography, chest scan, and colonography). It first analyzes the medical images (x-ray images, computerized tomography – CT scans, and magnetic resonance imaging – MRI) and uses a machine-learning algorithm to identify potential problems.

Traditionally, it takes a few days or even weeks for the doctors to review all the x-ray images before confirming lung cancer. Artificial intelligence scans

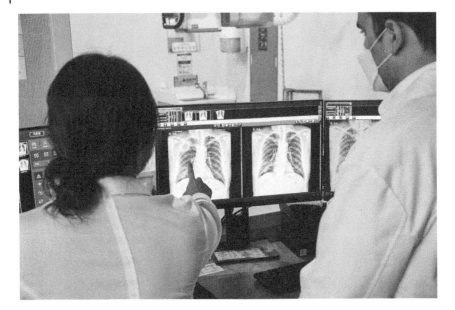

Figure 7.3 Radiology analysis. Source: Hale [69] / Questex LLC.

all the x-ray images within an hour. It mimics the human brain to process the data for decision-making and analyzes more complex patterns in medical images. It filters out the images and highlights the tumor area. It helps the doctors to detect and identify the subtleties linked with the tumor quickly. It speeds up the diagnostic process and improves overall efficiency. It significantly reduces the doctors' workloads and lets the doctors focus on the filtered images for cancer diagnosis. The patients can receive the treatment in the early cancer stage, which significantly increases survival chances. The medical imaging also tracks the tumor growth during the treatment, which alerts the doctor about the tumor size change to improve the treatment.

Artificial intelligence has massive potential advantages in medical imaging analysis but also faces big challenges. It relies on the neural network for prediction, and the model is trained using a custom dataset with bias and errors. It is still required the doctors to confirm the prediction results. Therefore, more data is fed into the model for training and improves the overall accuracy. Artificial intelligence also creates the diagnosis problem. If the system reports the patient has a 10% risk of cancer, it is difficult for the doctor and patient to decide to have surgery or not. It puts additional pressure on the doctor and defeats its original purpose.

7.4   Smart Medical Device

Artificial intelligence is integrated with smart medical sensors [71, 72] (Figure 7.4) to monitor patient health conditions. The patient wears the smart watch or wristband to record the vital signs (temperature, blood pressure, heartbeat, and sleep pattern), then sends the information to the doctors for monitoring. One of the key vital signs is the echocardiogram (ECG or EKG), which is a simple test to record the electrical activity of the heart and provides information about the heart rate and rhythm. The echocardiogram can show the enlargement of the heart due to high blood pressure, which leads to the risk of stroke. It can also detect atrial fibrillation (AF) from irregular heart rhythms, which results in a heart attack. Early detection is important because the patent can receive the treatment and increase survival chances. Otherwise, the disease progression may lead to life-threatening results. The echocardiogram results are also used to predict one-year mortality by comparing the prediction with the common disease pattern. The mortality risk can alert the patient to visit the specialist for further diagnosis, or more aggressive treatment is considered.

The smart medical device also records the patent's sleep patterns because it plays an important role in physical health. Healthy sleep protects physical and mental health with good quality of life. It keeps the body developing, conserves energy, boosts the immune system, and refreshes the mind. Poor sleep signals potential health problems, high blood pressure, heart attack, heart failure, stroke, and diabetes. The patent should consult with the doctor for sleep improvement.

Figure 7.4   Smart medical device [71]. Source: DenPhoto / Adobe Stock.

Regular blood pressure measurement is critical which keeps tracking the patient's health conditions. High blood pressure damages the blood vessels and results in stroke, heart attack, and heart failure. It also causes blurred vision, kidney failure, aneurysm, metabolic syndrome, and dementia. High blood pressure is the fifth leading cause of death in the United States.

The smart medical device is also applied for a diabetes analysis. The device can monitor the blood glucose level day and night. It sends the records to the doctor, who follows up with the patients with the right diet menu. It alerts the patient when the glucose level reaches a dangerous level. The patient uses the medication to lower blood glucose immediately. With a family history of diabetes, the medical device can monitor the patient's health conditions. When it identifies the diabetes symptoms, it alerts the patient to change the diet and visit the doctor to conduct further examination. It offers additional proactive care for the patient.

7.5 Electronic Health Record

Currently, the doctors spend 27% of their time seeing the patients and 49% of their time doing the paperwork, including EHR [73] (Figure 7.5). It is estimated the doctor shortage will reach 122 000 by 2030, and more and more doctors are leaving due to overload and burnout. The advance of artificial intelligence allows the doctor to capture patient communication through natural language processing (NLP). It can record the conversation and transcribe it into the correct EHR format, including

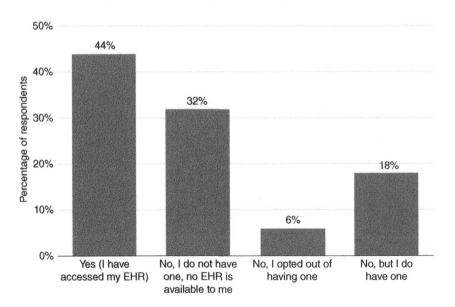

Figure 7.5 Electronic health record. Source: Jordan [73]. Statista.

the patient's health conditions and treatment plan. It saves the doctor huge effort and time on documentation. It relieves the pressure and reduces the turnover rate.

Artificial Intelligence also solves the medical record incompatible problem. It transfers the medical record from one hospital to another and automatically transforms the record into a different format. This approach is not limited to the United States but also extended to other countries. Suppose the patient travels from the United States to Mexico, it allows the patient to communicate with Mexican doctors through a smart medical device. The device translates the medical record from English to Spanish using NLP and lists out the patient history as well as the treatment plan. Mexican doctors can give the best care to the patient. The miscommunication delays the treatment and increases the life-threatening risk.

Artificial intelligence makes the healthcare administration more efficient; it enhances productivity with lower errors, improves operational efficiency, and reduces operating costs. However, it also faces ethical challenges, the patients' concern about how to ensure data security and protect personal privacy.

7.6   Medical Billing

Medical billing is a challenging process, which accurately translates the patent information into the standard code for billing. It is estimated the billing error resulted in $36.21 billion in 2017, according to the Centers for Medicare and Medicaid Services (CMS). Therefore, artificial intelligence is emerged to support medical billing [74] (Figure 7.6). The machine learning model is trained through the patient database with medical terminology and recognizes the medical term

Figure 7.6   Medical billing [74]. Source: mrmohock / Adobe Stock.

and the treatment information (i.e. drugs, operations, procedures), then utilizes NLP to analyze the patient record and identify the proper billing code. 3 M has applied the 360 Encompass Professional System to support more than 1700 hospitals for medical billing. One hospital shows the billing accuracy reaches 98%. However, medical billing still faces serious challenges with the complex medical standard, where the medical procedure definition is increased from 3824 to 71 924, and the billing code is increased from 14 025 to 69 823 based on the latest 10th revision of the International Classification of Diseases (ICD-10)

7.7 Drug Development

Asides from medical diagnosis, artificial intelligence plays a huge role in drug development. It is estimated artificial intelligence-driven early-stage drug discovery market [75] will reach $10 billion by 2024. Machine learning makes drug research and development better, faster, and cheaper (Figure 7.7). The United States currently funds most drug research, but the development is still a difficult long-term process. Pharmaceutical companies need to explore different molecular structures for new drug discovery and undergo extensive three phases of clinical trials, then get approval from Food and Drug Administration (FDA). It typically takes more than ten years to develop a new drug. One of the leading biopharmaceutical companies, Pfizer, works

Figure 7.7 Drug development. Source: Alamanou [75] / BPT Analytics LTD.

closely with IBM Watson. It applies machine learning to search for new immuno-oncology drugs. It can analyze enormous amounts of complex data, understand different types of criteria, and recognize the hidden molecular structures for new drug discovery. It outperforms the research scientists and speeds up drug development.

Artificial intelligence also applies NLP to accelerate the new drug discovery further. It can scan through millions of medical literature and genetic datasets to identify new molecular structures, then validate the molecular structure with the drug target. It replaces humans for new drug discovery at a low error rate and reduces the development from a few years to a few months only. Google AlphaFold 2 is a new artificial intelligence system which is used to predict structures of proteins of SARS-CoV-2, the causative agent of COVID-19 and then speeds up the new vaccine and drug development.

Moreover, artificial intelligence can also optimize drug production processes. It gathers valuable clinical data from different patients and assesses responses in various populations. It can predict the effect of the drug in a respective population before the delivery. It reduces the delay in clinical trials and gets fast-track approval from FDA. As a result, it significantly reduces the drug development cycle and the overall cost.

7.8 Clinical Trial

Clinical trial is a critical process for drug development due to its high cost with a low success rate (<10%). Artificial intelligence is emerged to automate clinical trials [76, 77] (Figure 7.8) in three areas: patient recruitment, clinical trial design, and optimization. NLP is extremely useful for the clinical trial; it recognizes the medical information for the machine learning model training using the clinical database (i.e. lab notes, statistical data, and patient records) and recruits the patients matched with the clinical trial criteria. It first identifies the patient with the particular disease, illness, and injury in the clinical database, then lists out the patient treatment and the side effects of the drug with similar ingredients. It also prompts a series of questions for the patients to determine the patient physical, mental, and geographic fit for the clinical trial. This approach significantly shortens the recruitment time and finds the right patient for the clinical trial. The software also encrypts patient information for privacy protection.

For clinical trial design, the software studies the past clinical trials and related medical records to identify the risk factors, then provides the recommendations for the clinical trial design. It divides the patients into different groups and examines the possible side effects, especially an allergy or volatile reaction toward the drug. Predictive analytics are also used to establish the best practice with the past operations and procedures to optimize the clinical trials. It is also used to predict the market demand and how likely the doctors prescribe the drug.

Figure 7.8 Clinical trial [76]. Source: totojang1977 / Adobe Stock.

7.9 Medical Robotics

Medical robotics [78, 79] serves different healthcare roles through robotic processing automation (RPA) (Figure 7.9). It works as the virtual administrative assistant to handle all the tasks. When the patent arrives for the appointment, it collects the personal details and insurance information for registration. It also helps the patent to schedule different appointments and laboratory examinations to avoid long waiting times. This approach can fully utilize the healthcare system resource and maximize the overall profit.

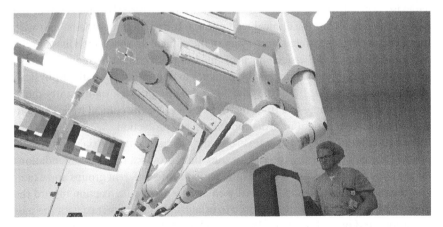

Figure 7.9 Medical robot [78]. Source: Mejia [78] / Emerj Artificial Intelligence Research.

Medical robotics also works as a clinical assistant, which accesses the patient record, medical history, examination results, and treatment plan. It analyzes all the data, then helps the doctor to diagnose and treat the patient. Based on the patient's health conditions, it can conduct statistical studies for predictive analysis. It reports the potential disease to the doctors and patients, then recommends prevention procedures and treatment plans.

Recently, the medical robot is extended to assisted robotic surgery with better control over the surgical operation, especially for vision assistants and robotic arm control. The heart surgeons apply the miniature robot, Heartlander, to enter the small incision on the chest to perform the mapping and therapy over the heart's surface. It reduces the physical trauma to the patient and speeds up the recovery. Although medical robots benefit healthcare development, the doctor must engage with the patients, families, and communities to understand their concerns toward robotic surgery. It is important to build up better trust between humans and machines.

7.10 Elderly Care

Aging is a serious problem; the number of people over 60 or above is expected to grow from 962 million in 2017 to 2.1 billion in 2050. Elderly care [80] becomes more important in the near future (Figure 7.10). It is difficult for caregivers and

Figure 7.10 Elderly care [80]. Source: Tyler Olson / Adobe Stock.

doctors to address the demand of elderly patients. With the emergence of artificial intelligence, smart medical devices monitor the elderly patient's vital signs and alert the potential health problems. It acts as a virtual medical assistant to facilitate care coordination and medication adherence; it answers any medical inquiries and schedules medical appointments. Moreover, it notifies the family about any home accidents (i.e. fall, stroke, and heart attack) to save the elderly patient's life.

7.11 Future Challenges

Artificial intelligence has already revolutionized the healthcare system with many advantages. It also faces a lot of challenges [81]. Artificial intelligence does not have emotions and feelings. It never shows sympathy toward the patients. Lack of communication makes the patient feels anxious about the illness. Unlike the machine, the doctor heals the sick and comforts the patient.

Artificial intelligence depends on the trained dataset to diagnose the patients and offer treatments. However, the dataset may not contain sufficient information about the patient with a particular medical background. It may introduce diagnostic errors and affect patient survival.

There is also an argument between healthcare providers and insurance companies: Who will pay for artificial intelligence used in healthcare? Artificial intelligence can offer the best treatment plan for the patient, but the treatment plan may be too expensive that the patient cannot afford it. The doctor can offer more affordable treatment for the patient.

Currently, the healthcare industry employs millions of workers and represents 17% of gross domestic production (GDP) in the United States. If artificial intelligence replaces many healthcare jobs, it will result in serious unemployment. Although the healthcare industry provides workers training programs, it takes time for the workers to adopt artificial intelligence in the workplace. The new position is not suitable for all workers. It still leads to job loss issues.

Exercise

1. Is telemedicine useful during a pandemic?

2. How can artificial intelligence avoid fault diagnosis?

3. How can artificial intelligence improve medical imaging analysis?

4. Can a smart medical device improve your health?

5. What are the challenges for EHRs?

6. How can artificial intelligence apply to medical billing?

7. What are the major benefits of artificial intelligence in drug development?

8. How can artificial intelligence enhance clinical trials?

9. Will you trust medical robotic surgery?

10. Will artificial intelligence solve elderly care in the future?

11. What are artificial intelligence challenges in the healthcare system?

8

Finance

In the era of artificial intelligence, the customer always asks, "Can I buy this today?" The virtual assistant [82, 83] responds to the inquiry and advises the customer for shopping. It analyzes the customer's current finances, updates the account information, and foresees the potential issues, overdrafts, shortfalls, and late fees. It helps to avoid overspending. Artificial intelligence also provides businesses with a wide range of benefits, such as fraud prevention, financial forecast, and stock investment. It analyzes a large amount of data in real-time and assists the business in making the right decision. It saves the company millions of dollars every year.

8.1 Fraud Prevention

According to the Digital Fraud Tracker, the total loss of the fraud is estimated at $4.2 trillion in 2018, and the fraudulent mobile application transactions are increased 680% between 2015 and 2018. With the rise of cyberattacks, artificial intelligence [84–87] plays an important role in enhancing cybersecurity for financial institutions, credit card companies, and insurance firms. It analyzes the data from millions of incidents, identifies the potential threats, and protects the network from cyberattacks (Figure 8.1).

The fraud prevention system first collects the customer's digital identity, such as an address, e-mail, phone number, spending behavior, payment history, and other data points, then creates the customer data records. It develops a regular transaction baseline and correlates the records with a legitimate transaction. It is based on digital identity to detect suspicious transactions in real-time.

Understanding Artificial Intelligence: Fundamentals and Applications, First Edition.
Albert Chun Chen Liu, Oscar Ming Kin Law, and Iain Law.
© 2022 The Institute of Electrical and Electronics Engineers, Inc.
Published 2022 by John Wiley & Sons, Inc.

Figure 8.1   Fraud detection [84]. Source: NicoElNino / Adobe Stock.

If it detects an abnormal transaction, it sends the customer a red flag warning. If the customer determines the transaction is fraudulent, it credits the customer's account and removes any transaction charges. Otherwise, the customer is responsible for paying any disputed amount and charges. The system further secures the transaction through biometric authentication, facial recognition, and fingerprint validation.

Artificial intelligence also learns from the mistakes and updates the fraud detection over time. If the system raises a red flag for a specific transaction without fraud, it feeds the legitimate transaction data for training and corrects the detection mistake. The fraud prevention system is continuously updated to improve detection accuracy. In the long run, the system can analyze false data automatically and identify money laundering or fraudulent transaction directly. It is not required to manually correct the mistakes and improve the system efficiency.

MasterCard has developed a fraud detection system called Decision Intelligence (Figure 8.2). It applies predictive analytics to analyze the transaction data based on records and determines whether the transaction is fraud or not. The system can detect abnormal shopping behavior through risk assessment, merchant information, geographic location, transaction time, and purchase type. This approach significantly reduces the chance of fraudulent transactions.

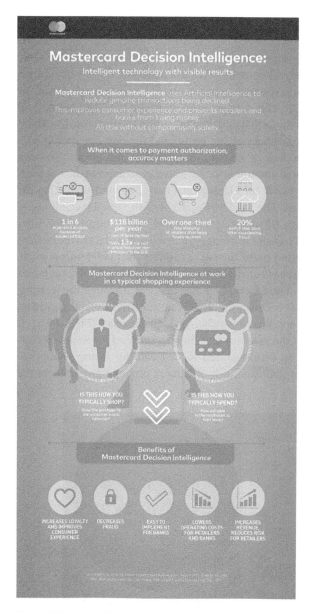

Figure 8.2 MasterCard decision intelligence solution [85]. Source: Mejia [85] / Emerj Artificial Intelligence Research.

8.2 Financial Forecast

Predictive analyses play an important role in business and government growth. Many companies [88–90] rely on complex software models to identify the market trends and forecast the future revenue, expense, and cash flow, which drives the business growth. However, it takes a huge effort and time to collect the data. It converts the data into the right format and then integrates the data into the financial forecast model. The drawbacks of the traditional forecast are timing consumption, insufficient data, lack of updates, human bias, and errors. Artificial intelligence can handle a large amount of structural or unstructured data. It feeds the data into the neural network for identifying, classifying, and predicting the financial trend and outcome. The model is updated with new data training to improve the overall accuracy (Figure 8.3). The model can be targeted for other market predictions through transfer learning, which feeds new data to the current model with different prediction goals. Instead of training the model from scratch, it fine-tunes the model and speeds up the training. It reduces the effort for complex software model development and focuses on data analysis. Through the learning process, the financial forecast becomes more accurate and drives business growth.

Amazon offers artificial intelligence tools, Amazon Forecast (Figure 8.4). It helps the company without the machine learning background for financial forecasting. The tool is based on historical and related data for future prediction. Compared with the current approach, it is 50% more accurate and reduces the

Figure 8.3 Financial forecast [88]. Source: Sergey Nivens / Adobe Stock.

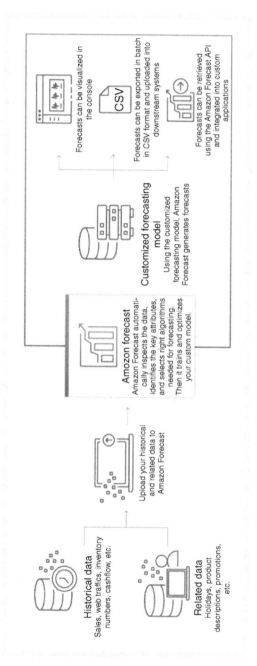

Figure 8.4 Amazon forecast. Source: Ref. [90] / Amazon, Inc.

forecasting time from a few months to a few hours only. All the results are fully encrypted to prevent data leaks. It helps the company make reliable and accurate finance forecasting.

Artificial intelligence is also used to maintain the financial stability of a country. It can process a huge amount of economic data in a short period and identify the financial triggers. Due to periods of high and low economic growth, global economic shocks are inevitable, and recessions are unavoidable. Both are parts of the boom-and-bust economic cycle. The government must provide a fiscal stimulus package to recover from the financial crisis and prevent the 1930s Great Depression from happening again. Artificial intelligence collects global economic data and estimates the natural disaster economic impacts. It predicts potential economic contractions and alerts the government at an early stage. The government can provide a centralized, timely response to financial crises, spur new forms of consumption, and recover from the recession.

8.3 Stock Trading

On the stock market, artificial intelligence [91–94] analyzes the investor financial situation, the risk tolerance, and investment objective, then suggests whether the conservative, moderate, or aggressive portfolio meets the investor demand (Figure 8.5). It makes the equity decision and suggestion to buy, sell or hold the stocks dependent on the investor risk tolerance.

Artificial intelligence analyzes the company financial statement, the sales report, and the company forecast to predict the stock price changes. It also considers the world economy, international politics, and climate change for stock market investment. It gives the best stock advice to the investors.

Artificial intelligence also predicts the stock price changes through social media (i.e. Twitter, Instagram, Facebook). It covers the product launch, the management changes, and the competition update. It further enhances the stock market prediction. Alpaca combines deep learning with high-speed data processing to provide a short-term and long-term stock forecast. It predicts market price changes and translates that information into multi-market dashboards for stock trading. It is partnered with Bloomberg to provide investors with short-term major market forecasts in the United States.

Kavout applies machine learning models with distributed computing to analyze a large amount of data in real-time (Figure 8.6). It is not limited to the historical stock data but also accesses related information from the news, blogs, social media, and analyst report. It correlates all the data for stock market prediction. It recommends the stock portfolio for investors, and the result outperforms the finance advisors.

Figure 8.5 Stock trading [91]. Source: bluebay2014 / Adobe Stock.

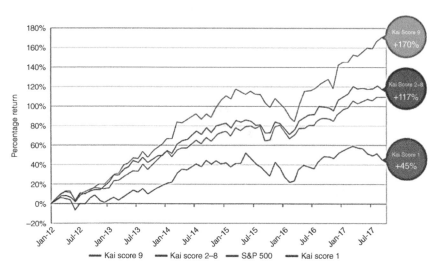

*Based on monthly rebalanced portfolios of stocks of S&P500. Transaction costs not included. Stocks are equally weighted. Past performance is not an indicator of future results.

Figure 8.6 Stock portfolio comparison. Source: Bharadwaj [94]. Kavout.

8.4   Banking

Artificial intelligence has a significant advantage in its multiple financial services roles [95–98] (Figure 8.7). Banks offer facial recognition for biometric authentication, which links up the customers' photos with the digital identity and stores them in the system database. It applies facial recognition to distinguish between the living human and the still image for identity verification. It can detect the falsified image and deny the customer's accounts access. This approach has been widely applied for automatic teller machine (ATM) and mobile applications.

Artificial intelligence chatbot becomes the virtual financial assistant, which communicates with customers and gives prompt and accurate responses. The virtual financial assistant covers different bank services, account inquiries, loan applications, and money transfers. The chatbot also transcribes the customers' conversations into the digital record. It reduces the burdens of paperwork and document handling with fewer errors.

The banks currently use the credit score for credit card application, which includes the active loans, payment records, and the number of active cards. This approach often delays the credit card application and results in ambiguity and uncertainty in decision-making. Artificial intelligence analyzes all customer information and financial records. It quickly identifies the fraud and denies the suspicious application. It significantly speeds up the credit card application process.

Artificial intelligence is also used for loan applications. It generates the customers' in-depth status reports and financial forecasts. The assessment of possible risks and the analysis of financial history allow the bankers to make loan

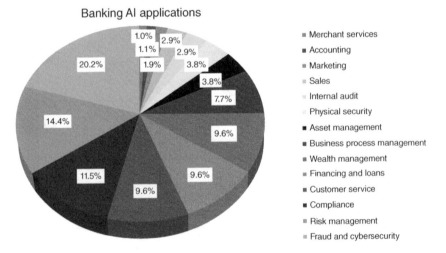

Figure 8.7   Banking AI product. Source: Based on Faggella [97].

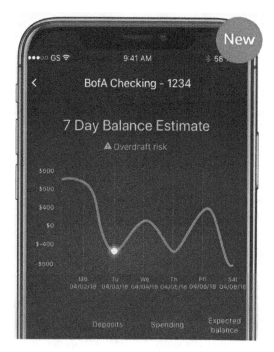

Figure 8.8 Bank of America chatbot: Erica [97].

decisions quickly and reduce the risk of bad debts. It leverages human and machine capabilities to drive operational and cost efficiencies. It allows banks to produce real-time optimal and personalized solutions based on available data.

Bank of America offers the chatbot, Erica, which answers the customer's questions and provides the account balance (Figure 8.8). It can provide past transaction records and refund confirmation. It reminds the customer about the received bill and recurring payment schedule. It also shows the weekly spending snapshot and alerts the overspending leads to negative balance through predictive analytics. It becomes an important virtual financial assistant for the customer.

8.5 Accounting

In terms of administrative management, artificial intelligence can perform many accounting tasks [99–102] (Figure 8.9) and enable the automation of the information-intensive process, such as monthly/quarterly close procedure, account payable/receivable, claim management, procurement process, and account audit through the natural language processing (NLP) approach. It can collect, store, and process financial

Figure 8.9 Accounting [100]. Source: Andrey Popov / Adobe Stock.

information and accounting data quickly and efficiently. Artificial intelligence offers accurate services to reduce the overall cost as well as human errors. It believes that artificial intelligence would handle many accounting tasks and shift the accounting professional's role to consulting and advisory in the future.

EY (formerly known as Ernst and Young) [103] applies artificial intelligence to capture important information from the contracts, such as lease commencement date, paid amount, renewal, or termination options. It automates the auditing through robotic process automation (RPA) and handles 70–80% simple lease contract review. It reduces a large amount of time spent on administrative paperwork. It allows the accountants to analyze different lease options and make the correct decision, bringing huge benefits to the company.

8.6 Insurance

Many insurance companies currently develop artificial intelligence applications [104–106] for underwriting, claim processing, and fraud detection. It is targeted to improve the turn-around time and reduce the operational cost (Figure 8.10).

Cape Analytics offers the service to analyze the property through satellite images for underwriting. It first fed millions of homes and buildings satellite images into the system for training. Each image is labeled with the

Figure 8.10   Insurance claims [104]. Source: Andrey Popov / Adobe Stock.

property attributes and conditions, such as roof, backyard, swimming pool, and surrounding environment. It analyzes the property satellite images and lists out the property estimation and condition. It helps the underwriter to make the correct underwriting decision.

Ant Financial, an affiliate of Alibaba Group, offers Ding Sun Bao software to recognize the vehicle damage and facilitate the claims. The application is trained through thousands of damaged vehicle images, which label the damage and the repair cost. The insurer uploads the damaged vehicle images to the system. The system searches for similar damage cases quickly in the database. It lists out the damaged parts, repair costs, and the accident impacts on the insurance. This approach can significantly speed up the claiming process.

Exercise

1. How does artificial intelligence apply to fraud detection?

2. How can we improve the financial forecast?

3. How does the virtual advisor help the customer for investment?

4. Will you trust artificial intelligence for stock trading?

5. How do you suggest to further improve stock prediction accuracy?

6. How does the banking system benefit from artificial intelligence?

7. What are the basic requirements for the virtual bank teller?

8. Will the accountant lose the job to the machine in the near future?

9. How does artificial intelligence improve the insurance claiming process?

9

Retail

During Thanksgiving, Black Friday, and Christmas, the shoppers wait in line outside the stores to buy gifts for family and friends. They hunt for the best deal on electronics, such as television, computer, game console, and mobile phone. Due to the high demand, shopping is no longer a hassle-free experience with many challenges, product scarcity, floating prices, and shopper competition.

Artificial intelligence is the new game-changing technology to simplify the shopping. It acts as a virtual shopping assistant to notify the shoppers about the stock availability, the store locations, the product warranty, the return policy, and the product reviews. It also analyzes the shopper's financial status and shopping wish list, then recommends the right product to the shoppers. It not only benefits the shoppers but also makes the retail stores profitable.

Currently, forty percent of companies use artificial intelligence to improve their business. With globalization and local proximity, more retailers choose to adopt artificial intelligence [107], which automates the operation, reduces the expense, increases sales, offers more product recommendations, and provides better customer services. Global spending on artificial intelligence will reach $7.3 billion in 2022 (Figure 9.1).

9.1 E-Commerce

Effective advertising plays an important role in business, which enables the retailer to attract more customers and compete with other companies. Artificial intelligence [108–110] further enhances E-commerce (Figure 9.2); it not only makes better advertisements but also simplifies the shopping. It first understands the customer profiles, which includes the demographic data and related information,

Understanding Artificial Intelligence: Fundamentals and Applications, First Edition.
Albert Chun Chen Liu, Oscar Ming Kin Law, and Iain Law.
© 2022 The Institute of Electrical and Electronics Engineers, Inc.
Published 2022 by John Wiley & Sons, Inc.

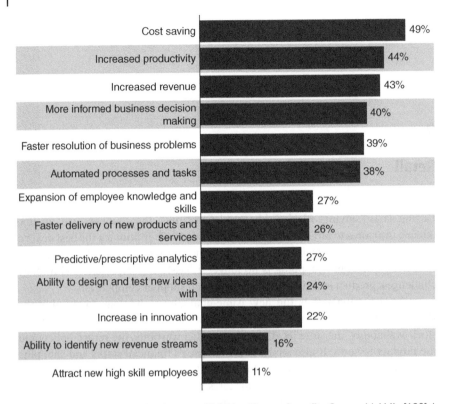

Cost saving 49%

Increased productivity 44%

Increased revenue 43%

More informed business decision making 40%

Faster resolution of business problems 39%

Automated processes and tasks 38%

Expansion of employee knowledge and skills 27%

Faster delivery of new products and services 26%

Predictive/prescriptive analytics 27%

Ability to design and test new ideas with 24%

Increase in innovation 22%

Ability to identify new revenue streams 16%

Attract new high skill employees 11%

Figure 9.1 Worldwide retail industry artificial intelligence benefits. Source: Makhija [108] / Guru Technolabs.

and explores the customer website browsing history and the past transaction records, then provides the product recommendations, enables faster checkout, and facilitates personal shopping with better customer service (Figure 9.3). Once the customer visits the website, it identifies the customers' needs and wants. It notifies the customers about the stock availability and provides the related products discount. It attracts the customers to make the purchase and increases the retail sales.

Crowdsourcing [111] is also widely used for e-Commerce product recommendations. It collects a large amount of data from different sources, then feeds the data into a model for training and applies for e-Commerce product search. If the customer searches the red rain boot for kids on the website, it first analyzes the sentence and identifies the product as "rain boot" not the "boot," which is targeted for the kids with smaller shoe sizes. With the description "red," it can quickly search for red rain boots in the kid catalog and provide the correct product recommendations.

Boomtrain is a scalable marketing artificial intelligence platform that collects customer data from multiple touchpoints like mobile applications, email campaigns,

Figure 9.2 E-commerce. Source: Makhija [108] / Guru Technolabs.

and websites. It analyzes the customer's online interactions and makes related product recommendations. Overall, artificial intelligence improves customer service and provides personalized recommendations. It allows the company to boost sales and profit. For example, the customer purchases the Kneron laboratory book on Amazon, he/she will get the matching hardware module recommended by artificial intelligence (Figure 9.3), which increases the retail sale and grows the revenue.

Artificial intelligence acts as a virtual shopping assistant, which response to all the requests and answers customer questions for better after-sale support. It notifies the customer about the delivery schedule and asks for a product review. If the customer wants to return the product, it simplifies the return procedure and understands the return reasons for quality improvement. It builds a strong relationship between the retailers and customers. Amazon adopts a similar approach for online shopping, and the overall sale is dramatically increased over the past few years.

Moreover, artificial intelligence also improves online shopping efficiency through conversion rate optimization (CRO). It converts the online visitors to customers through a website redesign, product photos, price display, and content arrangement. It successfully attracts the customer to purchase the product online.

9.2 Virtual Shopping

Artificial intelligence enables augmented reality (AR) and virtual reality (VR) [112–114] for virtual shopping. It allows the customer to explore different products in the immersive AR/VR environment. It focuses on the home improvement and retail fashion areas.

Look inside ↓

Kneron Computer Laboratory
Paperback – September 24, 2020
by Albert Chun Chen Liu Oscar Ming Kin Law (Author)

> See all formats and editions

Paperback
$16.88

2 New from $16.88

Kneron Computer Laboratory Workshop to accompany the KL520 USB dongle, https://www.amazon.com/dp/B087QTWVGT?ref=myi_title_dp

 Inspire a love of reading with Amazon Book Box for Kids
Discover delightful children's books with Amazon Book Box, a subscription that delivers new books every 1, 2, or 3 months — new Amazon Book Box Prime customers receive 15% off your first box. Learn more.

See all 2 images

Customers who viewed this item also viewed

KNEO Stem: AI module to build AI apps
$59.99

Figure 9.3   E-commerce product recommendation.

IKEA offers the mobile apps, IKEA Place (Figure 9.4), built on Apple's ARKit platform, which supports 2D/3D image recognition and tracking. The customer takes the room photos through the apps, then applies the AR capability to measure the room dimension. The customer selects the furniture from the IKEA catalog and drops it into the apps. The customer can move the furniture on the screen and fit it into different locations, then view the furniture from multiple angles.

For retail fashion, Fitnet develops the virtual fitting (Figure 9.5), which captures the customer's shape and size. The customer selects the clothes and accessories from the retail catalog, then displays them in the virtual mirror. The mirror also shows what the clothes look like when the customer moves around. It allows the customer to see how the clothes fit before purchase. The software

Figure 9.4 Home improvement. Source: de Jesus [112] / Emerj Artificial Intelligence Research.

Figure 9.5 Virtual fitting. Source: de Jesus [113] / Emerj Artificial Intelligence Research.

9.3 Product Promotion

Artificial intelligence is also widely used for product promotion [115] (Figure 9.6); it can determine the product relationship, the promotion impacts, pricing, and inventory control. If the customer buys the ground beef, it may affect the sale of the hamburger buns, or the pasta and tomato sauce. Once the promotion product is identified, artificial intelligence helps to forecast the sales and determine the price. It also predicts the drawback of the ground beef promotion, the sale of the hamburger buns may offset the sale of the hot-dog buns, resulting in a negative gain.

Figure 9.6 Product promotion [115]. Source: hxdyl / Adobe Stock.

To support the product promotion, it first collects the different products transaction history and the manufacturing cost; it also explores the past promotions and market campaigns results. Additional geographic data (i.e. store location) and competitor reactions are also considered to improve the overall promotion accuracy. Daisy intelligence works with the organic grocery store, Earth Fare to define the product promotion; the software Daisy AI understands the product relationship, promotion impacts, the competitor reactions, and the optimization goal (sales, margin, channel, supply, etc.), then determine the promotion strategy. Finally, it increases the top-of-line product sale by 3% and increases the promotion contribution from 20% to 40% for the total sales.

9.4 Store Management

Amazon launches innovative Amazon Go stores [116–118] (Figure 9.7) to reinvent the brick-and-mortar retail through "Just Walk Out" shopping. The customer just grabs and goes without checkout. Once the customer checks in the store, it individually tracks every person through the combination of multiple technologies, sensor fusion, person detection, object recognition, pose estimation, and activity analysis. It recognizes which items to pick up and drop off. It also distinguishes between different items being sold. All the items are linked to the virtual customer basket, then send the bill to the customers when they walk out of the store. It simplifies shopping with better inventory control and demand forecast. This innovation is the future of retail, and artificial intelligence is the source of innovation.

Figure 9.7 AmazonGo Store management [116]. Source: MariaX/Shutterstock.com.

Recently, the retail robot, Softbank pepper robot [119] (Figure 9.8), responds to customer inquiries and guides the customer to find the items inside the store. It also performs real-time inventory tracking, notifies the customers about the out-of-stock product, and improves the store's profitability. With Pepper Robot in California b88ta store, it increases 70% more visitors with 50% more sales.

9.5 Warehouse Management

Warehouse management controls and optimizes the entire warehouse operations, from the product entry into the warehouse until the product is sold, removed, or consumed. When the retailer receives the order, it picks up the item at the warehouse, packages the item, and delivers it to the customer. Warehouse management is a labor-intensive task with high operating costs. It is required a large number of laborers to work on the product delivery. Although artificial intelligence may not fully replace the current system, it can work in conjunction with human oversight to manage product delivery.

Amazon warehouse management system [120, 121] (Figure 9.9) depots over 45000 intelligent robots in different warehouses. They are used to stock up, count, and transfer inventory in the warehouses. The robot can deliver over 300 items/hours

Figure 9.8 Softbank pepper robot. https://softbankrobotics.com/emea/en/pepper. Source: Faggella [119] / Emerj Artificial Intelligence Research.

Figure 9.9 Amazon warehouse management. Source: tiero / Adobe stock.

Figure 9.10 Amazon Prime Air Drone [122]. Source: UPI / Alamy Stock Photo.

compared to 100 items/hours of human pick-up. It also works all day without a break to improve warehouse efficiency. Based on the statistical study, it saves over $22 million for every automated warehouse and accounts for 20% of operating costs.

Currently, Amazon further connects the warehouse with the delivery fleet through the Scout self-driving unit and Amazon Prime Air drone [122] (Figure 9.10) for product delivery. Scout self-driving unit has delivered the products in four locations around the United States. Amazon Prime Air can deliver up to five-pound packages to the rural area in under thirty minutes. Amazon invests in that respective artificial intelligence to increase delivery efficiency, minimize error, and maximize sales. The delivery fleet benefits the company with fewer delivery workers at a lower cost; it also autonomously delivers the products faster and cheaper than by car.

9.6 Inventory Management

Besides warehouse management, inventory control is also critical for business success. Inventory management means the right stock, at the proper levels, in the right place, at the right time, at the right cost, and at the right price. Excess inventory ties up the cash flow and affects daily operations, such as rental, salary, and general expenses. Insufficient inventory results in lost sales and costly back-ordering. Therefore, it is important to balance the inventory and cash flow.

Artificial intelligence [123–125] offers two major improvements over inventory management (Figure 9.11). First, it applies object recognition to scan the products on the shelves. It detects the low inventory stocks and quickly restocks the

Figure 9.11 Walmart inventory management. Source: Mejia [125] / Emerj Artificial Intelligence Research.

products. It also alerts the supply chain to schedule the shipment to fulfill the product demands. Second, it can incorporate external data sources, weather data, and utilize time series models to make demand forecast. The model predicts the sales of retail stores over a certain period. The store can stock at the right time and improve the profits. To avoid prediction error, reinforcement learning is also implemented to support decision-making.

9.7 Supply Chain

Artificial intelligence [126, 127] has advantages over the traditional supply chain approach for inventory control with demand forecast (Figure 9.12). It analyzes a large amount of data (inventory, sale, demand, and supply) and considers multiple factors and constraints to improve supply chain efficiency. It is easy to identify the inventory shortage and notify the product suppliers to schedule a delivery. It adopts a multi-sourcing strategy to meet the growing product demand during the shopping seasons (Back to school, Thanksgiving, and Christmas).

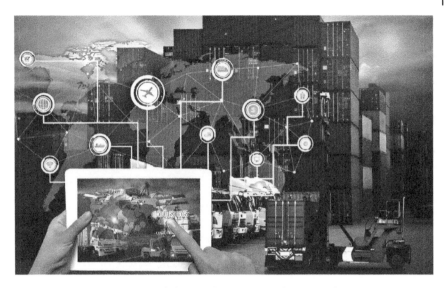

Figure 9.12 Supply chain [127]. Source: Travel mania / Shutterstock.

Even if inventory is being managed correctly, the products must be delivered to the customer efficiently and effectively. Currently, supply chain professionals spend a lot of time utilizing spreadsheets to devise delivery plans. Artificial intelligence offers cognitive automation, which automates route planning and overcomes delivery challenges without human interventions. It analyzes multiple data (i.e. weather, traffic, and road conditions), explores different routes, and then chooses the best delivery route using predictive modeling. United parcel service (UPS) uses an AI-powered global positioning system (GPS) to create the most efficient fleets' routes. It significantly speeds up the delivery and reduces the cost. Lineage Logistics applies artificial intelligence to forecast and predict when food orders will leave and arrive at their respective facilities. It shortens the transport time and keeps the food fresh.

Exercise

1. Can you describe the e-commerce changes within these few years?

2. What is virtual shopping?

3. How does artificial intelligence improve product promotion?

4. How does artificial intelligence change store management?

5. Will the retail robot replace the human?

6. How does Amazon change warehouse management?

7. What will future delivery and logistics change?

8. What is the role of artificial intelligence in inventory management?

9. How do you improve supply chain management?

10

Manufacturing

As the product demands increase, the factory capacities decrease, and the regulation policies tighten, there is an urgent demand for manufacturing adaptability. The machines can produce a massive amount of data, but the factory cannot use them to increase overall productivity. Besides the overwhelming demand, the factory also suffers from a high error rate, which prevents the introduction of high-quality goods and products. In recent years, manufacturing has adopted artificial intelligence to increase overall productivity and significantly reduce production errors.

For manufacturing, the investment [128–130] in artificial intelligence hardware, software, and services jumps from $2.9 billion in 2018 to $13.2 billion by 2025 (Figure 10.1). It reduces the production cost, improves the overall efficiency, and achieves better time-to-market advantages. The artificial intelligence market is projected to increase from $1.0 billion in 2018 to $17.2 billion by 2025, with a compound annual growth rate (CAGR) of 49.5% over the period (Figure 10.2). It shows the potential of artificial intelligence in manufacturing.

10.1   Defect Detection

Currently, many workers are forced to examine the differences between functional and defective components manually, which results in numerous false positives in production. It also reduces the overall revenue and efficiency. Fortunately, artificial intelligence can detect defects in production lines [130–132] using object recognition. It automates the visual inspection to find microscopic flaws in production. It can spot the defects quickly with high accuracy and efficiency compared with

Understanding Artificial Intelligence: Fundamentals and Applications, First Edition.
Albert Chun Chen Liu, Oscar Ming Kin Law, and Iain Law.
© 2022 The Institute of Electrical and Electronics Engineers, Inc.
Published 2022 by John Wiley & Sons, Inc.

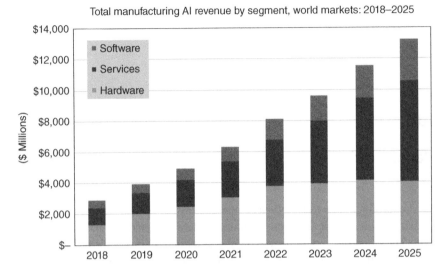

Figure 10.1 Artificial intelligence total manufacturing revenue [128]. Source: Omdia.

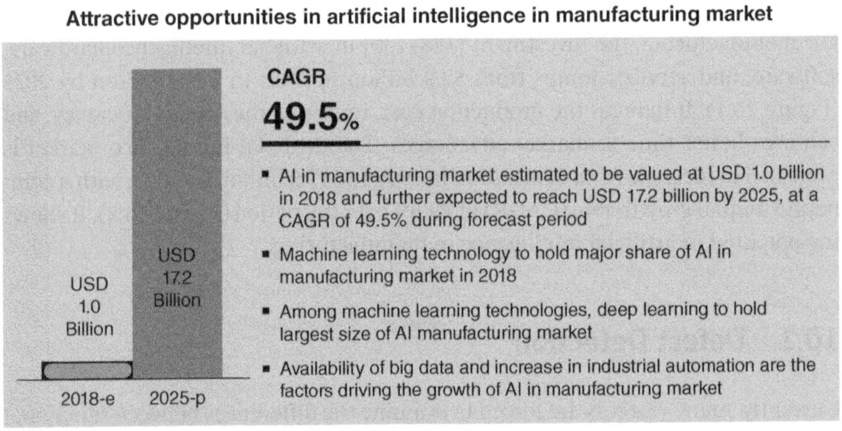

Figure 10.2 Artificial intelligence manufacturing opportunity. Source: Adapted from Columbus [130].

manual inspection (Figure 10.3). As a result, the false positive detections are dramatically reduced, the quality assurance is greatly improved.

Audi adopts artificial intelligence with visual inspection in the Ingolstadt press shop. It first trains the neural network through the thousands of images captured by the camera. Then it applies the machine learning model to identify the defective

Computer vision-based quality control in action

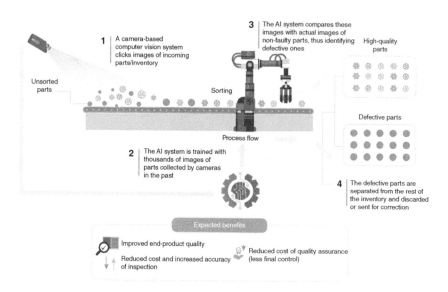

Figure 10.3   Defect detection. Source: Columbus [130]. Capgemini Research Institute.

part and separate it using the robotic arm. The production flow is fully automated, and the efficiency is highly improved.

10.2   Quality Assurance

Currently, the workers are forced to ensure the products are correctly manufactured with the proper components. Artificial intelligence [130, 133, 134] ensures all the parts are correctly configured and monitors any potential defective product through object recognition. Through artificial intelligence integration and optimization, it oversees the complex manufacturing process and identifies the problem immediately with a quick response. It dramatically improves manufacturing quality assurance.

Nokia introduces machine learning visual inspection (Figure 10.4). It alerts the production line worker if it detects production errors. The worker can correct the problem immediately to avoid the production outage, and it significantly reduces the manufacturing downtime. As a result, it achieves high-quality manufacturing with low production costs.

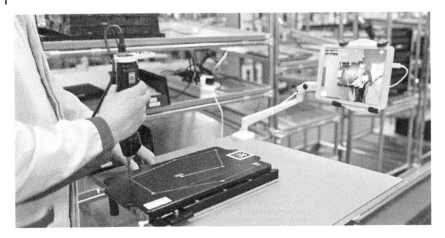

Figure 10.4   Quality assurance [130]. Source: Nokia.

10.3   Production Integration

Artificial intelligence [131, 135] also helps to integrate the production through data sharing and coordinate all the machine operations. When the machine is broken down, it first alerts the worker to repair the machine, then triggers the contingency plan to switch the workload from one machine to another to continue the operation. It avoids the production outage due to machine failure. Moreover, it also monitors the entire manufacturing process, such as the process lead time, raw material used, and production output estimation. It provides the factory with a valuable demand forecast for inventory control.

General Electric has launched Brilliant Manufacturing Suite, which connects all the equipment with the sensors, then monitors and tracks everything in the production line. The suite runs the diagnostics on the equipment and determines the condition of the machinery as well as the quality of the products. It is used to identify any issues and detect any inefficiencies. This approach improves the machine's effectiveness by 18%.

Artificial intelligence [136, 137] also optimizes the production line to automate the manual and repetitive tasks through the collaborative robot – Cobot (Figure 10.5). It learns the actions through manual movement rather than rule-based programming. It repeats the same action without actual programming. It saves the long setup time and easy targets for different operations. Fanuc [134, 135], the leading Japanese industrial robotics company, further extends intelligent robots to train through reinforcement learning. They perform the same tasks repeatedly to achieve the accurate target. It partners with Nvidia to further speed up learning through multiple intelligent robots. It replaces one robot eight hours

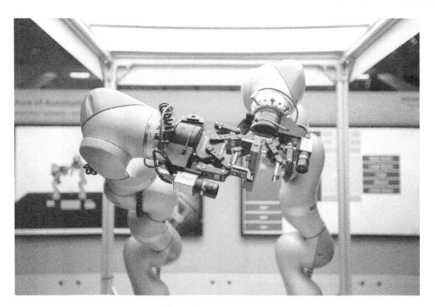

Figure 10.5 Collaborative robot (Cobot) [136]. Source: ©Siemens AG.

learning with eight robots one-hour learning. Fast learning means less downtime and handling more products in the same factory.

10.4 Generative Design

Generative design [130, 133] applies artificial intelligence to explore different alternatives to meet the product specification (Figure 10.6). It uses a machine-learning algorithm to learn which approach works and which does not. It feeds the raw material, cost constraints, functional requirements, manufacturing methods, and other parameters into the machine learning model to optimize the design. It provides the company with different alternatives that were not traditionally available. It is a time-consuming process to explore the alternatives with a large number of parameters manually. It provides high-quality products at a lower cost. It also simplifies the complex manufacturing process and speeds up production. Therefore, it significantly increases the company revenue.

General Motors collaborated with Autodesk to implement the generative design approach to design seatbelt brackets. It explores over 150 different designs through machine learning and finally converts the eight components design into a single

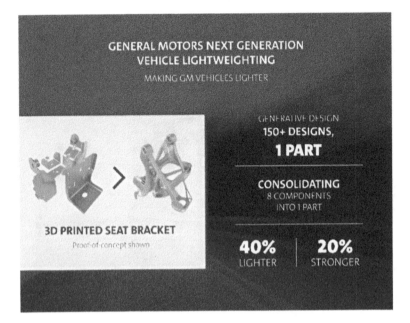

Figure 10.6 Generative design. Source: Harvard Business Review.

bracket. It is 40% lighter and 20% stronger than the original one. It reduces not only the production cost but also the manufacturing cycle.

10.5   Predictive Maintenance

Artificial intelligence also reduces manufacturing downtime through predictive analysis [130, 133] (Figure 10.7). It avoids equipment breakdown and monitors the production process. It runs the production line over a thousand times during the trial tests, then collects the data from all the machines and predicts the failure modes. It corrects the manufacturing errors before the actual production. It also allows the factory to explore different manufacturing processes to increase overall productivity.

General Motor mounts the camera on the assembly robot and analyzes the image to predict the robot's failure. During the pilot run, it detected 72 instances of component failure across 7000 robots. It identified the potential loss before the unplanned outages. It avoids production outages and significantly improves the overall efficiency.

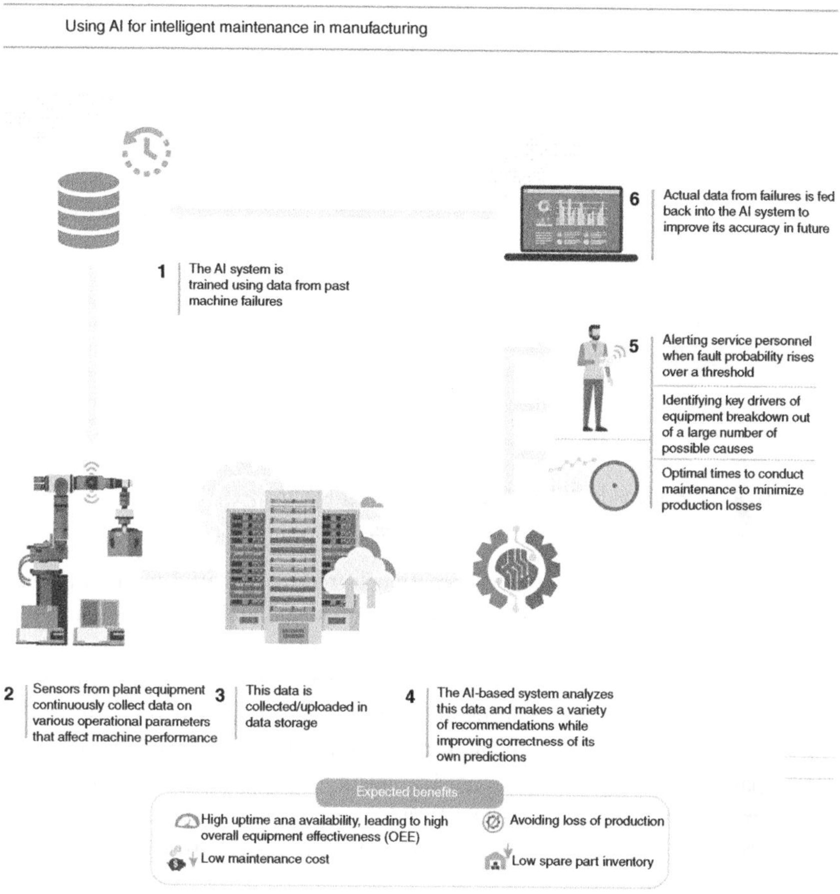

Using AI for intelligent maintenance in manufacturing
1 The AI system is trained using data from past machine failures
2 Sensors from plant equipment continuously collect data on various operational parameters that affect machine performance
3 This data is collected/uploaded in data storage
4 The AI-based system analyzes this data and makes a variety of recommendations while improving correctness of its own predictions
5 Alerting service personnel when fault probability rises over a threshold
Identifying key drivers of equipment breakdown out of a large number of possible causes
Optimal times to conduct maintenance to minimize production losses
6 Actual data from failures is fed back into the AI system to improve its accuracy in future
Expected benefits
High uptime ana availability, leading to high overall equipment effectiveness (OEE)
Avoiding loss of production
Low maintenance cost
Low spare part inventory

Figure 10.7 Predictive maintenance. Source: Columbus [130]. Capgemini Research Institute.

10.6 Environment Sustainability

Artificial intelligence not only transforms the manufacturing workplace but also mitigates climate change. Currently, many factories seriously harm the environment; they consume a large amount of energy, exhaust the raw materials, pollute the air, and produce harmful plastic. Artificial intelligence substitutes traditional materials with sustainable ones through green technology and significantly reduces toxic plastic production. It replaces fossil fuels with renewable energy (solar or wind energy) to prevent environmental damage. It also optimizes the

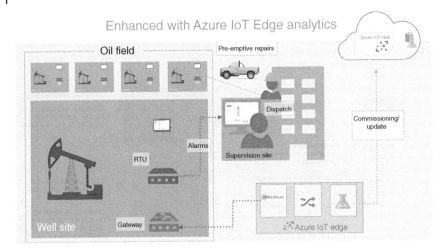

Figure 10.8 Sustainability [130]. Source: Scheneider Electric.

manufacturing process through automation to reduce material waste and high energy consumption. It achieves environmental sustainability through artificial intelligence.

Schneider Electric [130] develops the internet of things (IoT) analytics solution based on the Microsoft Azure machine learning approach (Figure 10.8). It selects the optimal machine learning models and tunes the model parameters to predict mechanical failure. It improves workplace safety and decreases maintenance costs. Moreover, it avoids the production outage for machine restart, reduces chemical waste, and achieves the environmental sustainability goal.

10.7 Manufacturing Optimization

Artificial intelligence also optimizes the manufacturing workflow in different areas [130, 136] (Figure 10.9). It can define the high-level prediction with machine models from the template library, then optimize the machine deployment to improve the overall productivity. It also applies the machine learning algorithm to improve defect detection, manufacture throughput, sustainability, and production yield. Manufacturers can predict the demands to prioritize the production, simplify the supply chain and fulfill the custom product demands. It significantly increases the company profits

Figure 10.9 Manufacture optimization [136]. Source: Land Rover MENA / Wikimedia Commons / CC BY 2.0.

Exercise

1. How does defect detection improve the production yield?

2. How do you compare the human to the machine for quality control?

3. How do you further improve the product quality?

4. What is the benefit of generative design?

5. How do you apply the intelligent robot for production?

6. How does predictive analysis improve manufacturing productivity?

7. How do you improve the manufacture to minimize the environmental impact?

8. What is the benefit of manufacturing optimization?

11

Agriculture

In developed and developing countries, agriculture is the backbone of the economy, which is the important income source of the rural communities and employs millions of workers. In some countries, agriculture is the primary income source and represents a major component of the gross domestic product. As the global demands for crops are increased, and climate change impacts are exacerbated, traditional farming is no longer a sustainable long-term solution. The world's population will reach 9.7 billion by the end of 2050, but an additional 4% of the land is available for cultivation only. Food production cannot keep up with the demand. The effects of temperature changes, droughts, and floods can make farming unsustainable, accelerating soil erosion or depleting the water supply. Thus, artificial intelligence [138, 139] starts a new agricultural revolution (Figure 11.1). It allows people to modify the environment to harvest crops quickly and efficiently. It also monitors soil conditions, performs pest control, and makes accurate weather predictions. It would drastically increase food production and boost the global economy.

11.1 Crop and Soil Monitoring

Currently, deforestation and deficiencies in soil represent significant threats to food production. Artificial intelligence [59, 140] applies the machine vision to identify possible soil deficiencies, understand the soil defects, and detect plant pests and diseases (Figure 11.2). Smallholder farmers apply smartphone apps to correlate foliage patterns with certain plant diseases. These apps capture visual information, such as damaged leaves, soil color, and plant shape, to help farmers manage their crops. It provides a low-cost solution to increase food production on a small farm.

Understanding Artificial Intelligence: Fundamentals and Applications, First Edition.
Albert Chun Chen Liu, Oscar Ming Kin Law, and Iain Law.
© 2022 The Institute of Electrical and Electronics Engineers, Inc.
Published 2022 by John Wiley & Sons, Inc.

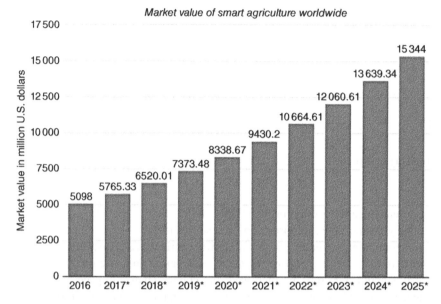

Market value of smart agriculture worldwide

Figure 11.1 Smart agriculture worldwide market. Source: Columbus [130] / IDAP.

Figure 11.2 Crop and soil monitoring. Source: de Jesus [59] / Emerj Artificial Intelligence Research.

For larger farms, drones are widely applied to improve overall food productivity. The drones are equipped with a camera, sensors, and global positioning system (GPS), which produces detailed 3D field maps with terrain, drainage, soil visibility, and irrigation. A multispectral camera is further used to capture more information than a standard camera. It analyzes soil conditions, measures plant growth, and detects the disease. It creates an unprecedented increase in food production. The drone covers a vast amount of land quickly and efficiently through the aerial view. It provides high-quality images with precise position through GPS technology.

The drone provides a simple alternative to defect the soil defect and track the plant growth progress. It also protects the workers' safety and prevents the workers from collecting the data under dangerous conditions. The drone can fly over challenging terrain or around the obstacle for data collection. The farmers can fly the drone much faster than walking; it covers more areas at a higher speed. The drone can help the farmers save money on labor costs and collect more precise data to improve overall productivity. The agricultural drone market is expected to grow significantly in the near future.

Gamaya applies machine learning and crop science with a hyperspectral imaging camera to analyze the soil's strengths and weaknesses (Figure 11.3). It provides a detailed soil content summary, including the pathogen screening with bacteria, fungi, and microbial evaluation. The hyperspectral imaging camera can capture 40 bands of color; it is ten times better than the standard camera, which captures four bands of color only. The plants reflect the light differently with various physiologies and characteristics. It produces the corn leaves chemical maps based on the spectral images. It shows the farmer how to improve the soil condition with a precise

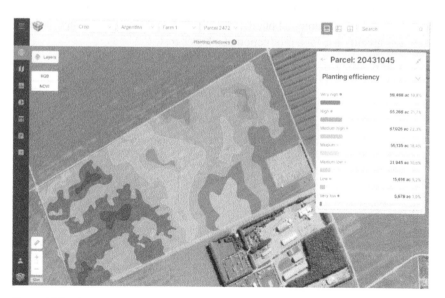

Figure 11.3 Corn leaves chemical maps. Source: https://www.gamaya.com/solutions/soyfit.

fertilizer and recommends the seeds based on the soil conditions. It also monitors the presence of weeds and insect diseases, which alerts the farmers for pest control. These approaches significantly improve productivity to increase profit.

11.2 Agricultural Robot

Agricultural robots [141–143] automate harvesting and replaces most labor-intensive farming (Figure 11.4). It increases food production by picking up fruits better and cheaper than the workers. Harvest CROO Robotics introduces a strawberry picking machine, which can pick the strawberries across eight acres of land within 24 hours. It is comparable to 30 farm workers with an annual cost of $676 200.

With the autonomous vehicle advances, it speeds up the development of the self-driving tractor. The self-driving tractor is used for plowing to cultivate the soil, which prepares the seed sowing or planting. With preset routes and obstacle detection, the tractors are programmed to move towards dedicated areas with obstacle collision avoidance. One supervisor can control many self-driving tractors. It speeds up the plowing operations and allows the workers to perform other tasks on the farm.

Harvest Automation develops an HV-100 robot to handle the highly repetitive and strenuous work of spacing crops and plants in the greenhouse (Figure 11.5). It prevents the worker from working under high temperatures and pristine environments to grow ornamental plants, specialty fruits, and veggies. It significantly increases greenhouse food production at a lower cost.

Figure 11.4 Agricultural robot. Source: Sennaaar [141] / Emerj Artificial Intelligence Research.

Figure 11.5 Greenhouse farming robot. Source: Gossett [142] / Built In.

11.3 Pest Control

The increased use of herbicides becomes a critical issue for weed herbicide resistance. It accounts for a $43 billion loss based on the Weed Service of America report in the United States. Artificial intelligence helps farmers to protect crops from weeds using agricultural robots [144] (Figure 11.6). These robots employ machine vision to spray herbicides with high precision and reduce the amount of herbicide sprayed onto crops. Blue River Technology has started utilizing a robot to spray weeds on cotton plants, preventing herbicide resistance. Uncontrolled weed results in millions of losses every year, the pest control becomes the top priority for the farmers.

Accenture develops artificial intelligence tools, PestID, which allows pest control technicians to identify bugs from the images. It applies machine learning to search the pest database and recognize the bugs, then recommends the plan include the proper chemical and approach for bugs treatment. It significantly saves the farmers' time and money.

11.4 Precision Farming

The goal of precision farming is profitability, efficiency, and sustainability. It is summarized using the phrase, "Right Place, Right Time, Right Product." It replaces the labor-intensive, repetitive farming procedure using artificial intelligence. It identifies

Figure 11.6 Pest control. Source: Bisen [144] / Medium.com.

the soil conditions and crop diseases, classifies the root causes, quantifies the impacts, and then predicts the outcome. It is useful for agricultural yield management. With the support of artificial intelligence [145, 146], the farmers can collect thousands of predictive data regarding weather patterns, water usage, or soil conditions through the Internet of Things (IoT) devices, humidity sensors, wind sensors, and soil thermometers (Figure 11.7). The system runs through millions of possible scenarios. It

Figure 11.7 Precision farming [145]. Source: William W. Potter / Adobe Stock.

helps farmers to determine the best crop choices. The system gives farmers suggestions that the seed choices with the combination of resources will produce the most successful results. It provides better seasonal food production.

Precision farming is used to create seasonal forecasting models to predict weather patterns and improve food production. Machine learning model connects with satellites provides the farmers with a billion points of agronomic data daily, including temperature, wind speed, precipitation, and solar radiation. It can detect rotational movement in clouds and identify shapes of clouds that may lead to storms or periods of rainfall. The major advantage of these predictive models is that they predict the weather a month in advance. Thus, the farmers can make correct decisions on how to manage the production.

The international Corp Research Institute for Semi-Arid Tropics (ICRISAT) works with Microsoft to improve productivity. It collects 30 years of climate data with real-time weather data to determine the optimal time to plant, ideal sowing depth, soil fertilization, and irrigation control. This approach can significantly increase the production yield to fulfill the demand.

Exercise

1. Why are crop and soil conditions important for agriculture?

2. Why are drones applied for soil and crop monitoring?

3. How do drones improve food productivity?

4. How does artificial intelligence improve agriculture robot development?

5. Will the agriculture robot replace the human worker?

6. How do you apply artificial intelligence for pest control?

7. What do you suggest for improving precision farming?

12

Smart City

As the global population rapidly increases, the demand for urban services inevitably outplaces current supply rates. The city infrastructure cannot keep up with the growing population. Without further development, the cities will face enormous infrastructure strains, worse traffic congestion, poorer sanitation, higher crime rates, and bigger environmental problems. The adoption of artificial intelligence and the internet of things are necessary for future "smart cities" development [147–150]. New York and Taipei [151] are transformed into the prosperous city [152], and they leverage artificial intelligence and internet of things to improve the quality of life (Figure 12.1). Artificial intelligence benefits city developments, including smart transportation, smart parking, waste management, smart grid, and environmental conservation.

Even though the smart city represents a promising development, it is not easy to collaborate with other government agencies to work together. The governments and cities must establish a central agency to work across various departments and coordinate different developments. A second concern is data security and personal privacy. The local cities should improve data transparency, which first obtains public consent about the data collection and explains the uses of data. It limits information sharing among different agencies. The smart city must also develop an information security system to prevent data leaks and cyberattacks.

12.1 Smart Transportation

The smart city improves transportation and reduces traffic congestion through adaptive signal control. The smart transportation system [153–157] (Figure 12.2) installs the traffic camera and roadside sensors to monitor the road conditions,

Understanding Artificial Intelligence: Fundamentals and Applications, First Edition.
Albert Chun Chen Liu, Oscar Ming Kin Law, and Iain Law.
© 2022 The Institute of Electrical and Electronics Engineers, Inc.
Published 2022 by John Wiley & Sons, Inc.

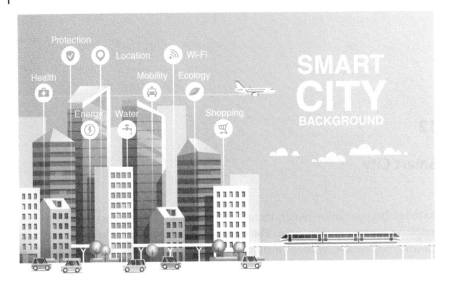

Figure 12.1 Smart city [151]. Source: faber14 / Adobe Stock.

Figure 12.2 Smart transportation. Source: P. Publishing [153] / Packt Publishing Limited.

then reports the traffic information to the traffic management system (TMS) in real-time. Artificial intelligence analyzes the data and adjusts the traffic flow through traffic light control. It changes the traffic light to allow more vehicles to pass and reduce the vehicle's waiting time. It can resolve the traffic congestion during the rush hour. Moreover, it reports traffic signal malfunction and any car accident, then alerts the driver about the road condition to avoid traffic congestion. This approach significantly reduces the traveling time. San Diego has installed 12 adaptive traffic systems on the busiest road to control the traffic flow. It successfully reduces travel time by 25% and decreases the number of vehicle stops up to 53% during the rush hour. It dramatically improves the overall traffic flow.

Artificial intelligence allows public transit such as buses, subways, and trains to communicate and send the updated schedule to the public through the smartphone. It alerts the public of any schedule changes and reduces the public wait time. It also analyzes the data to suggest the new transit routes and increase the public transit services. It encourages the public to switch from driving to public transit to reduce traffic congestion.

12.2 Smart Parking

One transportation breakthrough is smart parking [153–155] (Figure 12.3), which embeds the sensors into the parking spots and parking garage. They detect the position of all available parking spots and identify if the parking spot is vacant or occupied. It notifies the drivers how many parking spots are available. The drivers no longer struggle to find parking spots in select areas. It not only reduces driving stress but also saves traffic time. Moreover, it reduces the number of vehicles on the road as well as traffic accidents.

In Redwood City, VIMOC installed the vehicle detection sensors in two of the city's large parking garages. The parking space information not only displays outside the garages but also notifies drivers through the smartphone. The driver knows where the parking spot is available, and they do not waste time finding the

Figure 12.3 Smart parking [153]. Source: Vectorpouch / Adobe Stock.

parking spot. It improves traffic flow and provides essential information for future city planning.

12.3 Waste Management

The smart city also focuses on climate change mitigation to reduce greenhouse gas emissions for environmental protection. Despite green technology, tax incentives, and political legislation, emissions are rapidly increasing, and climate change may be inevitable soon. One possible solution is waste management [153, 154] (Figure 12.4), which installs sensors on waste bins to detect the waste level. If the waste bin is full, it notifies the waste management system to dispatch a garbage truck for waste collection. Barcelona's waste management system employs a similar approach for garbage truck dispatch. It reduces the number of truck dispatches and effectively collects the waste.

Moreover, artificial intelligence applies machine vision to differentiate paper, plastic, glass, and waste food items. It identifies the reused or recycled items to improve the overall recycling efficiency. It helps to achieve the goal, reduce, reuse, and recycle, then creates a sustainable environment.

12.4 Smart Grid

The smart city utilizes the smart grid [158, 159] (Figure 12.5) to supply electricity to the public. Artificial intelligence monitors the energy sources to regulate the power supply and usage. The energy sources are no longer limited to fossil fuels or nuclear power plants. It also considers the distributed renewable energy source,

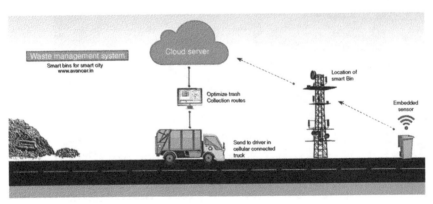

Figure 12.4 Smart waste management. Source: From [153] / Packt Publishing Limited.

Figure 12.5 Smart grid [159]. Source: jamesteohart / Adobe Stock.

especially solar energy. In the United States, the solar energy supply has tripled since 2010 (Figure 12.6).

The smart grid replaces the large regional grid with the microgrid. It applies artificial intelligence to manage the local electricity distribution between the

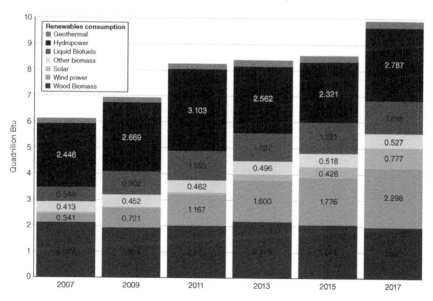

Figure 12.6 Renewable energy source. Source: Wolfe [158].

renewable energy source and fossil fuels electricity generation. It avoids long-distance power transfer because it contributes over 15% transmission loss. Google has applied a similar approach to data center operation. It significantly reduces the total power consumption and saves millions of dollars every year.

The smart grid can also predict any power outage due to machine failure and severe weather conditions (i.e. thunderstorms or freezing rain). It maintains grid stability and builds resilience for the future. The smart grid reduces electricity consumption and leads to substantial benefits.

12.5 Environmental Conservation

The World Health Organization (WHO) estimated 92% population lived in an air-pollution environment and resulting in over three million death every year (Figure 12.7). Smart city [160, 161] applies artificial intelligence to monitor air quality through air pollution sensors. It identifies the pollution sources and then regulates the traffic, construction, and manufacture to improve the air quality. It also shares real-time information with the public through the smartphone and alerts them to take protective measures, especially allergic patients. Dependent on the pollution level, it reduces the negative health impacts by 3%–15%.

Water is an important natural resource. Through the smart meter, the smart water system can track the water consumption pattern and notify the public about high water usage. It reduces about 15% water consumption in high water usage residential areas. The leak sensors can detect pipe leaks and alert the city for pipe repair. It significantly reduces the water loss by 25% and conserves the important natural resource, water.

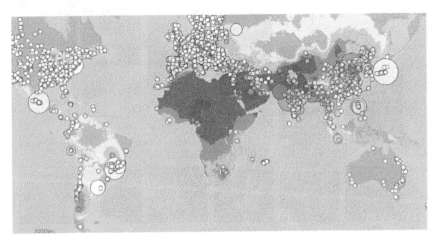

Figure 12.7 Air pollution map (WHO) [160].

Exercise

1. Will smart transportation solve traffic congestion?

2. How does the smart car support the current transportation system?

3. How does smart parking reduce driver's stress and save driving?

4. How can you improve waste management?

5. Will the smart grid fulfill the electricity demand?

6. How does artificial intelligence protect the environment?

7. What is the role of local government in smart city development?

13

Government

Why does artificial intelligence work for the government [162, 163, 164]? In the United States, the federal government employs more than 2.1 million civil servants and costs over \$168 billion. Artificial intelligence can help the government to manage the workforce more effectively and reduce expenses. It is estimated to save over 96.7 million to 1.2 billion federal hours annually with a potential cost of \$3.3 billion to \$41.1 billion. Moreover, the federal government has digitized over 225 million pages of the document and reaches 500 million pages by 2024. It is easy for artificial intelligence to handle a large amount of data and reduce the overall workload. Over 20 countries[1] have already implemented the national artificial intelligence strategy for future development (Figure 13.1). Artificial intelligence is estimated to increase the overall Gross Domestic Product (GDP) by 14% in 2030.

The artificial intelligence integration is further divided into three operating phases, assisted, augmented, and autonomous intelligence.

- Assisted Intelligence applies the big data approach, cloud computing, and data science to support decision making.
- Augmented Intelligence integrates machine learning over the current system to relieve the heavy workload and let the workers focus on other important tasks.
- Autonomous Intelligence automates the daily task through the robotic process automation (RPA) approach.

During the integration, the government should consider how to fully utilize artificial intelligence through detailed planning and reallocate the workload between humans and machines to avoid conflict. The government also trains the workers to adopt artificial intelligence in the workplace and improve overall efficiency.

---

1 The countries include United States, United Kingdoms, Canada, China, India, Germany, France, Russia, Japan, and South Korea.

Understanding Artificial Intelligence: Fundamentals and Applications, First Edition.
Albert Chun Chen Liu, Oscar Ming Kin Law, and Iain Law.
© 2022 The Institute of Electrical and Electronics Engineers, Inc.
Published 2022 by John Wiley & Sons, Inc.

Figure 13.1 Country national AI strategy. Source: Eggers and Beyer [163].

This chapter briefly describes several government artificial intelligence applications, including information technology, human service, law enforcement, legislation, and ethical issues. Finally, it covers the public perspective toward artificial intelligence.

13.1 Information Technology

13.1.1 The Power of Data

Since the information systems vary among the government departments and they are not compatible with each other. The civil servants spend a large amount of time and effort handling data transfer between different departments. However, the tasks are easily achieved through artificial intelligence [165, 166], which completes time-consuming tasks quickly and accurately, especially for routine jobs.

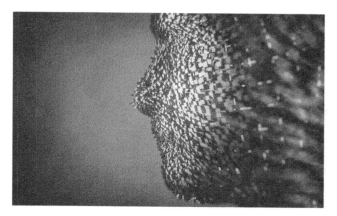

Figure 13.2 The power of data [166]. Source: gremlin / Getty Images.

It can extract valuable information from collected data and distribute them to the proper departments for data processing. The success of data integration unlocks the potential of the government for future development (Figure 13.2).

The government also applies artificial intelligence to understand the public demand in healthcare, education, public transit, and city planning, and it helps the government to allocate the resource to improve the living conditions. The government collects the traffic data from the road camera and sensors, then adjusts the traffic signal to improve the traffic flow and increases rush-hour public transit service to solve the traffic congestion problems. Through artificial intelligence, the government shifts the focus from reaction and remediation to prevention through predictive models and results in the prosperous city's growth.

13.1.2 Cybersecurity

Artificial intelligence also focuses on national security and prevents the cyberattack [166–168] (Figure 13.3). It incorporates the e-mail monitor software to detect anomalies and suspiciousness for a timely response. It identifies the network's

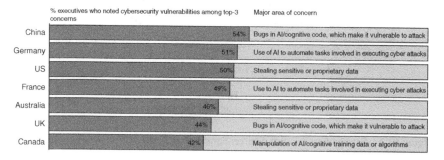

Figure 13.3 Cybersecurity. Source: Ramachandran [168].

malicious activities to prevent confidential data leaks. It also builds up the defense system against cyber-terrorist attacks, which alerts the system administrator that cyber terrorists infiltrate the network to steal the information, sabotage the operations, and damage the software or hardware.

13.2 Human Service

13.2.1 Casework Challenges

Currently, artificial intelligence is widely applied to human services [169, 170, 171, 172] to address the caseworker challenges (Figure 13.4). The caseworkers spend over 50% of the time handling the paperwork. Artificial intelligence reduces

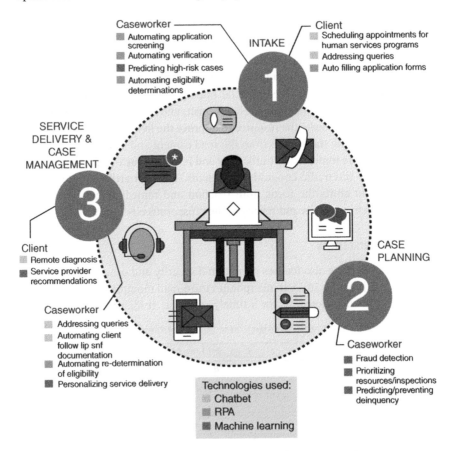

Figure 13.4 Caseworkers support. Source: Eggers et al. [169].

the caseworker administrative burden through natural language processing (NLP). It performs the speech-to-text operation and transcribes the information to different forms, then distributes the forms to other departments for further processing. It frees up the caseworkers and lets them spend more time with the clients. It also prioritizes high-risk cases to speed up service delivery and reduce the long waiting time.

Moreover, it overcomes the language barrier through language translators and communicates with non-English speaking clients. It is no longer to require the interpreter to help the clients with translation; it greatly increases the efficiency and reduces the cost. RPA can schedule the appointment and automate the client verification. It relieves the caseworkers' stress and lets them stay on the job to reduce the turnover rate.

13.2.2 High-Risk Prediction

In the United States, the Department of Human Services has applied artificial intelligence to predict high-risk cases [169, 170]. It targets children less than three years of age with young parents, mental health records, or abuse histories. It alerts the frontline caseworkers about high-risk cases and lets them investigate the claim based on the risk factor rather than the random sampling. It can prevent child abuse and neglect through high-risk prediction.

13.2.3 Fraud Detection

Artificial intelligence also alerts the potential fraud [169, 170]; it is based on past benefit records to train the neural network for fraud detection. It flags fraudulent applications so that the caseworkers do not waste time investigating false alerts and focusing on the actual fraud. The system can be updated with more records to improve the prediction, and it finally reaches 95% accuracy.

13.2.4 Virtual Assistant

Virtual assistants [169, 170] (Figure 13.5) overcome the language barrier to answer the client's general inquiry and allow the caseworkers to address more complex questions. Artificial intelligence can help the clients to determine eligibility from the government service and submit the application. It significantly speeds up the process and reduces the human service workload.

Figure 13.5 Virtual assistant. Source: Eggers et al. [169] / Deloitte.

13.3 Law Enforcement

Artificial intelligence played an important role in law enforcement, especially in crime prevention and detection. This chapter briefly describes several important breakthroughs in law enforcement.

13.3.1 Facial Recognition

For law enforcement, facial recognition [173, 174] is one of the critical technologies (Figure 13.6). It is no longer limited to surveillance but also crime apprehension. New facial recognition can change the facial appearance with glass, beard, hair, and dressing to identify the criminal. It also predicts the action based on facial emotion and body gestures to detect the individual intention, especially for shoplifting and suicide.

New York Department of Motor Vehicle (DMV) applies facial recognition to link up the ID photos and identification information. It alerts law enforcement for identity mismatches and successfully reports over 4000 fraud arrests related to identity theft.

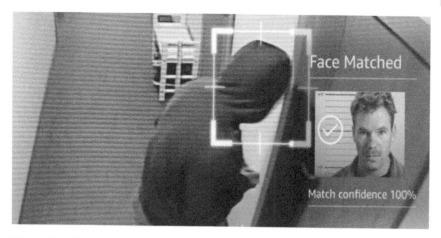

Figure 13.6 Criminal recognition. Source: Bump [174] / Emerj Artificial Intelligence Research.

Law enforcement also applies facial recognition software to find the missing people. In Northern California, law enforcement finds the missing people through Amazon Rikognition Integrated Traffic Jam software. The photos of missing people are uploaded to the system, and the software searches the database to find the highest matching scored image with geographical location. Finally, law enforcement successfully finds the missing people and arrests the suspect.

13.3.2 Crime Spot Prediction

Artificial intelligence combines with big data to predict when and where the crime is likely to occur [175, 176] (Figure 13.7). Based on the past criminal data, it clusters the crime type in time and space. Observing the recent burglaries and predicting when future burglaries will likely happen because the burglaries in one area may correlate with more burglaries in the surrounding regions shortly. This technique is called real-time epidemic-type aftershock sequence crime forecasting. It alerts the police to patrol heavily in crime spots for crime prevention. One success story is Tacoma, Washington; the burglaries are dropped by 22% after adopting the Predpol system for crime forecast.

13.3.3 Pretrial Release and Parole

In the past, the judges decided to release or set bail toward the criminal suspects based on their judgment. The judges must determine whether the suspects are a flight risk, dangerous to society, or risk toward the witness. It is a difficult task with human bias and error. Currently, the new system can predict if the suspects

Figure 13.7 Crime spot prevention. Source: Faggella [175] / Emerj Artificial Intelligence Research.

are low, medium, or high risk. It helps the judges to make the right decision. The system [175] (Figure 13.8) is based on a neural network, which feeds the criminal data into the training system. It calculates the risk factor for bail decisions with the suspect information. The system can also be updated for accuracy improvement through continuous criminal record feeding.

13.3.4 Augmenting Human Movement

Augmenting human movement [175] is derived from the movies and video games to create the programmatically generated human action with a different dress in different places. It is helpful for police to re-create the crime scene to convince a suspect to participate in a crime during an interrogation.

13.4 Homeland Security

Since 9/11, the United States government has formed the Department of Homeland Security (DHS) to protect the nation from terrorist attacks. It first carries out border security through the Customs and Border Agency (CBP). With 328 ports of

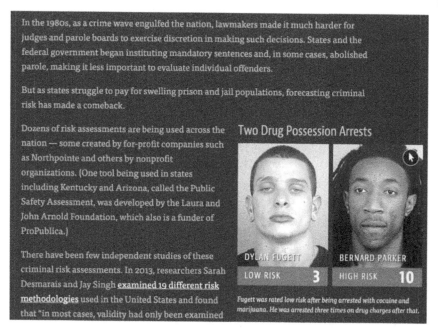

In the 1980s, as a crime wave engulfed the nation, lawmakers made it much harder for judges and parole boards to exercise discretion in making such decisions. States and the federal government began instituting mandatory sentences and, in some cases, abolished parole, making it less important to evaluate individual offenders.

But as states struggle to pay for swelling prison and jail populations, forecasting criminal risk has made a comeback.

Dozens of risk assessments are being used across the nation — some created by for-profit companies such as Northpointe and others by nonprofit organizations. (One tool being used in states including Kentucky and Arizona, called the Public Safety Assessment, was developed by the Laura and John Arnold Foundation, which also is a funder of ProPublica.)

There have been few independent studies of these criminal risk assessments. In 2013, researchers Sarah Desmarais and Jay Singh examined 19 different risk methodologies used in the United States and found that "in most cases, validity had only been examined

Two Drug Possession Arrests

DYLAN FUGETT   BERNARD PARKER
LOW RISK   3   HIGH RISK   10

Fugett was rated low risk after being arrested with cocaine and marijuana. He was arrested three times on drug charges after that.

Figure 13.8   Risk assessment [178].

entry and over millions of travelers, the machine learning approach [177] is required to improve the overall efficiency.

CBP explores the global travel assessment system (GTAS) developed by Tamr (Figure 13.9); it screens the travelers using advance passage information (API) and passager name record (PNR) to confirm the traveler's identity and identify the suspected one through the biographic data (name, gender, date of birth, citizenship, country of residence), travel data (number of passengers, frequent flyer, loyalty program, baggage detail), and flight information (carriers, routes, travel date).

The transportation security administration (TSA) also test the Apex screening at speed (SaS) program to analyze the images from multiple perspectives to screen the banned items and the treat objects (Figure 13.10).

13.5   Legislation

Currently, most governments have regulated new laws toward artificial intelligence. It takes time for the government to understand how the new technology is used or abused. Due to the rapid growth of artificial intelligence, the government takes time

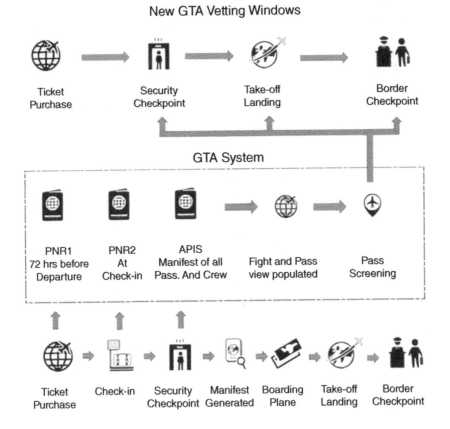

Figure 13.9 GTAS integrated workflow. Source: Adapted from Abadicio [177].

to enact the legislation. Therefore, the "soft law" is introduced; it is not enforced by the government but related to the professional guideline, code of conduct, and the standard. It allows artificial intelligence to develop without tight restrictions.

13.5.1 Autonomous Vehicle

One crucial piece of legislation is related to the autonomous vehicle [178–180]. Since the autonomous vehicle is driven side-by-side by pedestrians, the accident may introduce a deadly result. Twenty countries and regions have defined the permissive law for autonomous vehicles, and eight other areas are currently in discussion to put the autonomous vehicle into action. In the United States, federal

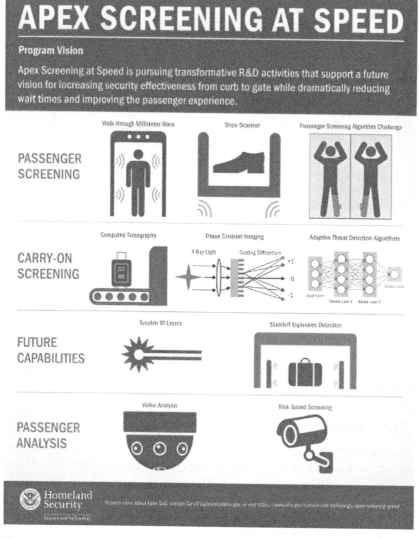

Figure 13.10 Apex screening at speed program. Source: Abadicio [177] / U.S. Department of Homeland Security / Public domain.

lawmakers and regulators work with the Department of Transportation to investigate how to regulate autonomous vehicles with new traffic laws. Over 60% of state government has legislated autonomous vehicle testing or deployment. Moreover, the new traffic laws also define who is responsible for the accident, the automotive maker or the driver. It is crucial for insurance coverage and compensation.

Figure 13.11   Data privacy. Source: Callahan [180] / Rev.com.

13.5.2   Data Privacy

The other important artificial intelligent legislation is data privacy [178–180] (Figure 13.11). The artificial intelligence predicts the customer shopping behavior and preference through online shopping, then recommends the sale. It also monitors or tracks an individual through either public transit or driving records. This approach seriously invades the public personal privacy; therefore, thirty-one countries and regions have issued prohibitive laws to restrict data sharing or exchange without prior consent or other restrictions.

13.5.3   Lethal Autonomous Weapons

Lethal autonomous weapons [178] are also under the law regulation. Smart weapons can automatically detect, track, and engage humans with lethal fires. It also achieves a more than 70% hit rate with a moving target. The military drone (Predator) is widely used for target killing on the battlefield. Currently, the law enforces human involvement in autonomous weapon development because it is linked to civil safety and national security.

13.6   Ethics

The rapid growth of artificial intelligence in the workplace raises a wide range of ethical issues [181, 182] (Figure 13.12). The public starts to address various ethical concerns regarding model transparency, bias and discrimination, personal privacy, system accountability, and worker displacement.

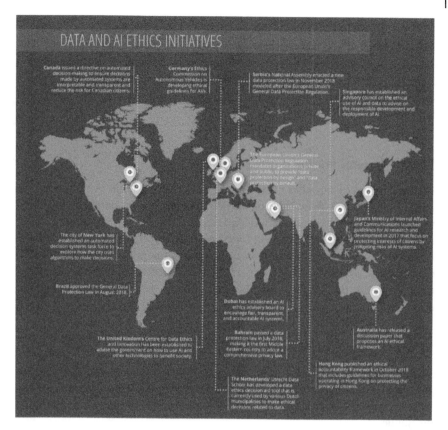

Figure 13.12   AI ethics. Source: Dalmia and Schatsky [181].

13.6.1 Data Monopoly

Big companies (i.e. Google, Metaverse, Amazon, and Baidu) collect large amounts of data and gain business advantages in the market through data analysis. Small companies don't access enough data to explore business opportunities. The government must extend current regulations: antitrust and competition laws for data management, which provides the chance to share the data among the small companies.

13.6.2 Model Transparency

Artificial intelligence is derived from neural network models, but they are not well understood or explained clearly. It is treated as a black-box model to predict the result. The public may question the results of the prediction, especially for the justice system and immigration decisions. The government is responsible for making the system transparent to the public and eliminating the public's misunderstandings.

13.6.3 Bias and Discrimination

As artificial intelligence becomes more powerful, the public worry about the ethical risks. Since the neural network model is trained from the dataset, the result is highly dependent on the data assumption and bias (gender, racial, and social status). The government must be aware of the data integrity and regulate the dataset for training.

13.6.4 Personal Privacy

Personal privacy is another critical issue related to artificial intelligence. The public is concerned about their privacy; they do not prefer personal data sharing among different government departments. Law enforcement applies facial recognition to identify the suspect for crime prevention and track the criminal. However, it may invade public privacy. The government must legislate for data collection as well as usage. It protects personal privacy and builds up better trust between the public and the government for artificial intelligence development.

13.6.5 System Accountability

Since artificial intelligence further automates the decision-making process, the government must define the process to monitor the system's accuracy and account for the system's reliability. It avoids mitigating the negative impacts from the public.

13.6.6 Workforce Displacement

Artificial intelligence automates the task and replaces the workforce; the government must consider reallocating the current workers to other job positions. The new training program is required to train the workers to adopt the latest technology in the workplace. New job positions should also be developed to accommodate the workers; otherwise, it creates severe unemployment and social problems.

Finally, the government must play an essential role in establishing policies and guidelines to regulate ethical issues. The government set up the central committee, which invites the researchers, developers, and representatives from different artificial intelligence integration areas. It also explains and resolves any questions to avoid conflict between the public and the government.

13.7 Public Perspective

The public [183] supports the government's artificial intelligence strategy but varies among the use cases. They are summarized as follows:

- The public supports artificial intelligence in information technology, human service, and law enforcement applications but not the sensitive decisions related to the justice and immigration system (Figure 13.13).
- In less-developed countries (China, India, and Indonesia), the public show strong support toward artificial intelligence but not the well-developed ones (Switzerland and Austria) (Figure 13.14).
- The age groups and geographical locations show different supports for artificial intelligence. The youth and those who live in the city demonstrate great support

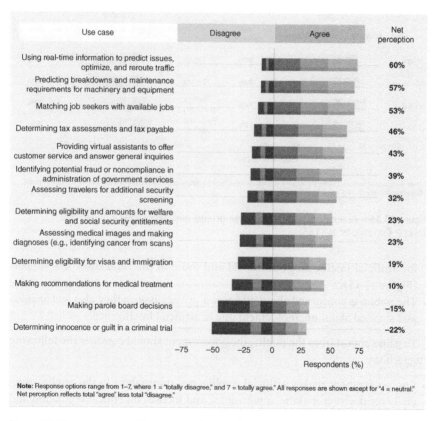

Figure 13.13   AI support with use case. Source: Carrasco et al. [183].

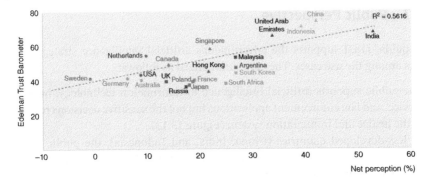

Figure 13.14 AI support with trust among different countries. Source: Carrasco et al. [183].

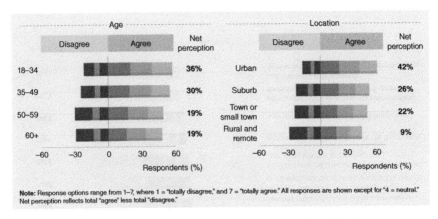

Note: Response options range from 1–7, where 1 = "totally disagree," and 7 = "totally agree." All responses are shown except for "4 = neutral." Net perception reflects total "agree" less total "disagree."

Figure 13.15 AI support with various age groups and geographical locations. Source: Carrasco et al. [183].

for artificial intelligence but the old and those in the rural show less support (Figure 13.15).

- The public is concerned about ethics and privacy issues; they also feel anxious and stressed about unemployment due to artificial intelligence.

To gain support from the public, the government should consider the following suggestions

- The government makes artificial intelligence transparent to the public, especially for decision-making applications, and focuses on ethical regulation and data privacy issues, then builds the trust between the public and the government.
- The government focuses on unemployment related to artificial intelligence. The government clearly shows the artificial intelligence transition process and re-trains the workers to adopt new technology. New job positions should be planned to accommodate the workers (Figure 13.16).

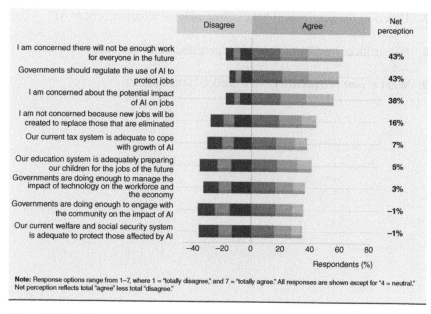

Figure 13.16 AI support with employment. Source: Carrasco et al. [183].

Since artificial intelligence evolves rapidly, the government should acquire experts for planning, transition, and educational program. The experts also help lawmakers to regulate artificial intelligence development.

Exercise

1. How does artificial intelligence benefit information technology?

2. What are the significant artificial intelligence contributions toward human services?

3. How can you further enhance artificial intelligence for law enforcement?

4. Which artificial intelligence should be legislated or regulated?

5. What are the major ethical issues related to artificial intelligence?

6. What is your suggestion for the data privacy protection?

7. How does the government handle the employee retraining due to AI?

8. Will artificial intelligence introduce new discrimination issue?

9. What is your perspective toward artificial intelligence?

14

Computing Platform

This chapter discusses different artificial intelligence computing platforms [16], including Intel central processing unit (CPU), Nvidia graphics processing unit (GPU), Google tensor processing unit (TPU) – cloud servers, and Kneron neural processing unit (NPU) – Edge artificial intelligence (AI) system. They serve various artificial intelligence hardware platform developments.

14.1 Central Processing Unit

Traditionally, the CPU is targeted for general-purpose computation; it is evolved from single instruction single data (SISD) architecture to single instruction multiple data (SIMD). It employs multiple processor cores (2, 4, 6, 8, or 16 cores) to support multi-thread processing for parallel computation. However, it cannot fulfill deep learning-intensive computational requirements. In 2017, Intel developed new Xeon scalable processor architecture (Purley platform) [184, 185, 186] to support the latest artificial intelligent development.

- Support 28 physical cores per socket (56 threads) at 2.5 GHz and up to 3.8 GHz at turbo mode.
- Six memory channels support up to 1.5 Tb 2.66 GHz DDR4 memory.
- 1 Mb private cache (L2 cache) and 38.5 Mb shared cache (L3 or Last-Level Cache – LLC).
- Operate at 3.57 TFLOPS (FP32) up to 5.18 TOPS (INT8) per socket and max 41.44 TOPS (INT8).
- Vector engine supports 512 bits wide Fused Multiply Add (FMA) instructions.

Understanding Artificial Intelligence: Fundamentals and Applications, First Edition.
Albert Chun Chen Liu, Oscar Ming Kin Law, and Iain Law.
© 2022 The Institute of Electrical and Electronics Engineers, Inc.
Published 2022 by John Wiley & Sons, Inc.

The major artificial intelligent enhancements:

- Skylake Mesh Architecture.
- Intel Ultra Path Interconnect (Intel UPI).
- Sub Non-Unified Memory Access Clustering (SNC).
- Cache Hierarchy Changes.
- Lower precision arithmetic operations.
- Advanced Vector Extension (AVX-512).[1]
- Math Kernel Library for Deep Neural Network (MKL-DNN).

New Xeon processor broke the record that trained the ResNet-50 model in 31 minutes and the AlexNet model in 11 minutes. Compared with the previous generation Xeon processor, it accelerates the ResNet-18 model training by 2.2x and inference by 2.4x.

14.1.1 System Architecture

In the previous generation, the Intel Xeon processor (Grantley platform) connects the CPU cores with peripherals using Intel quick path interconnect (QPI) ring architecture, which allows one-to-one data transfer only. As the number of cores increases, the memory latency is significantly increased. Intel Xeon scalable processor (Purley platform) solves the issue with the UPI mesh architecture, which can connect the processors in many different ways and provides multiple data transfer rates at 10.4 GT/s using a new packetization format (Figures 14.1–14.4).

The computer system is partitioned into two local domains connected with SNC. Each domain supports half of the processor cores and memory banks. It allows the system to schedule the tasks effectively and enable the memory for optimal performance resulting in better cache utilization. It significantly increases the overall hit rate to reduce the memory latency as well as mesh interconnect demands.

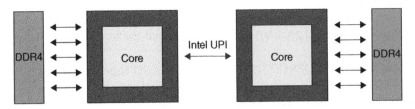

Figure 14.1 Two-socket configuration. Source: Adapted from Mulnix [186].

---

1 New Vector Neural Network Instruction (VNNI) in 2nd generation Intel Xeon scalable family

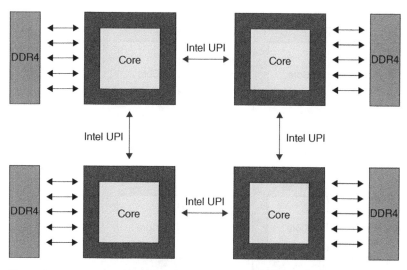

Figure 14.2 Four-socket ring configuration. Source: Adapted from Mulnix [186].

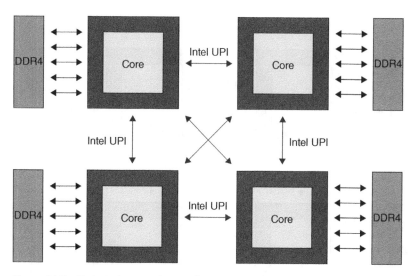

Figure 14.3 Four-socket crossbar configuration. Source: Adapted from Mulnix [186].

14.1.2 Advanced Vector Extension

Intel offers Advanced Vector Extension 512 (Intel AVX-512) [187] (Figure 14.5), which supports two floating-point FMA units as well as high (32 bits)/low (8 bits) precision multiply-and-add operations. Additional AVX-512_VNNI (Vector Neural Network Instruction) further simplifies FMA operations; both 8 bits

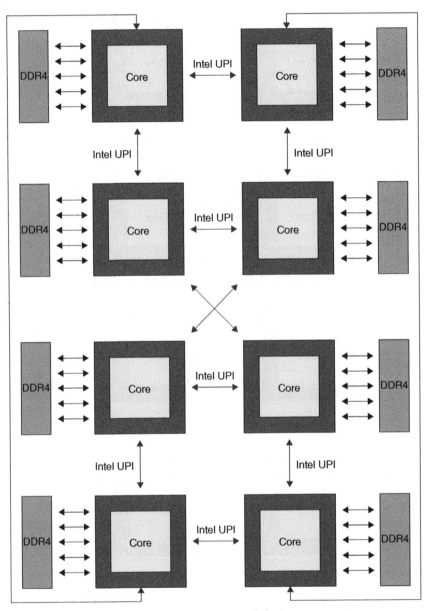

Figure 14.4 Eight-socket configuration. Source: Adapted from Mulnix [186].

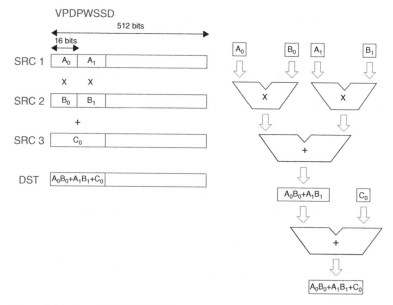

Figure 14.5 Intel AVX-512_VNNI FMA operation (VPDPWSSD). Source: Adapted from Ref. [187].

(VDDPBUSD) and 16 bits (VPDPWSSD) instructions perform multiply and add operation within a single cycle.

Advanced Vector Instruction (AVX-512) key features:

- Two 512 bits FMA instructions.
- Vector Neural Network Instruction (VNNI) supports.
- 512 bits floating-point and integer operations.
- 32 registers.
- Eight mask registers.
- 64 bits single-precision and 32 bits double-precision FLOPS/Cycle (with two 512 bits FMA).
- 32 bits single-precision and 16 bits double-precision FLOPS/Cycle (with one 512 bits FMA).
- Embedded rounding.
- Embedded broadcast.
- Scale/SSE/AVX "promotions."
- Native media byte/word additions (AVX512BW).
- High-performance computing double/quadword additions (AVX512DQ).
- Mathematic Transcendental support (i.e. π).
- Gather/scatter.

14.1.3 Math Kernel Library for Deep Neural Network

Intel MKL-DNN is optimized for deep learning computation. The key features are prefetching, data reuse, cache blocking, data layout, vectorization, and register blocking. It supports the inner product, convolution, pooling (maximum, minimum, average), activation (Softmax, ReLU), and normalization. It also modifies the routines for low precision (8 bits) inference to achieve the same accuracy at a higher speed.

14.2 Graphics Processing Unit

GPU consists of massively parallel Processing Elements (PEs) designed for computer graphics and image processing. In recent years, it is also targeted for artificial intelligent development (image classification, speech recognition, and autonomous vehicle), especially for neural network training. Nvidia Turing architecture [188] (Figure 14.6) accelerates the neural network training and inference to 14.2 TFLOPS. It also resolves the memory bottleneck with high-speed NVLink2 and 2nd generation High Bandwidth Memory (HBM2), which increases the data transfer rate to 900 Gb/s.

Nvidia Turing architecture (GeForce RTX-2080) key features are listed as follows:

- Six Graphics Processing Clusters (GPC)
- Each GPC has Texture Processing Clusters (TPC) with two Streaming Multiprocessor (SM) per TPC.
- Total 34 TPC and 68 SM.

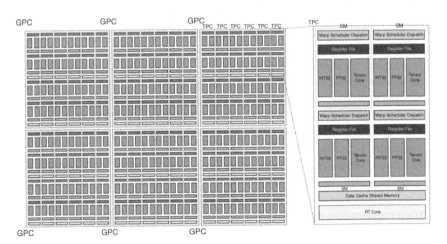

Figure 14.6 Nvidia GPU Turing architecture. Source: Adapted from Ref. [188].

- Each SM has 64 Compute Unified Device Architecture (CUDA) Cores, 8 Tensor Cores, and an additional 68 Ray Tracing (RT) Cores.
- GPU clock speed: 1350 MHz.
- 14.2 TFLOPS of single-precision (FP32) performance.
- 28.5 TFLOPS of half-precision (FP16) performance.
- 14.2 TIPS concurrent with FP, through independent integer execution units.
- 113.8 Tensor TFLOPS.

14.2.1 Tensor Core Architecture

New Tensor core (Figure 14.7) can perform $4 \times 4 \times 4$ matrix multiply and accumulate (MAC) operations; it multiplies two matrices simultaneously using the simultaneous multi-threading (SMT). It performs 16 bits floating-point multiplication and accumulates 32 bits floating-point partial sum. It significantly speeds up the overall performance of 16 bits floating point (8X), 8 bits integer (16X), and 4 bits integers (32X). It is much better than the previous generations, Pascal [189] and Volta [190] architectures.

14.2.2 NVLink2 Configuration

NVLink2 allows direct load/store between CPU and GPU memory (Figures 14.8–14.11). Each link provides 40 Gb/s peak bandwidth between 2 GPUs. NVLink2 is arranged in two different ways: GPU-to-GPU and GPU-to-CPU configurations.

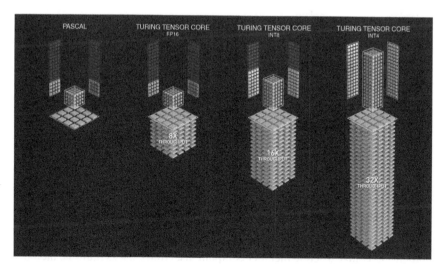

Figure 14.7 Tensor core performance comparison [188]. Source: Image courtesy of NVIDIA.

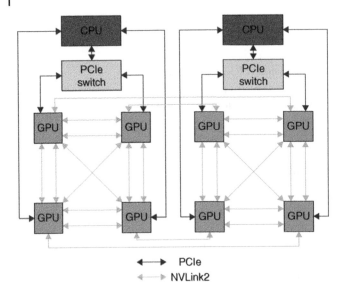

PCIe
NVLink2

Figure 14.8 NVLink2 Eight GPUs configuration. Source: Adapted from Ref. [189].

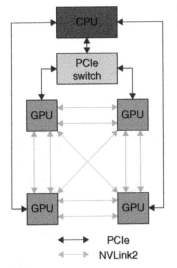

Figure 14.9 NVLink2 four GPUs configuration. Source: Adapted from Ref. [189].

PCIe
NVLink2

14.2.3 High Bandwidth Memory

Nvidia Turing architecture employs HBM2 (Figure 14.12) to resolve the memory bottleneck. Unlike discrete memory components, HBM2 stacks multiple memory dies together using Through Silicon Via (TSV) to eliminate the input/output pads. It significantly speeds up the data transfer at low power.

Figure 14.10 NVLink2 two GPUs configuration. Source: Adapted from Ref. [189].

Figure 14.11 NVLink single GPUs configuration. Source: Adapted from Ref. [189].

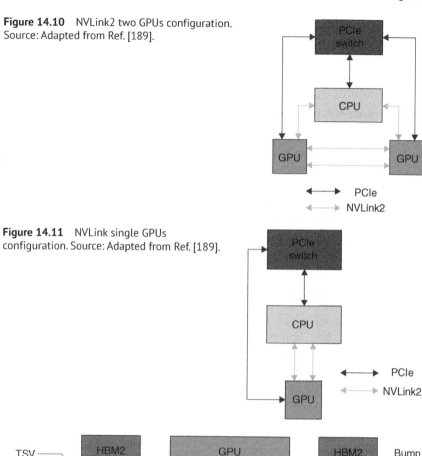

Figure 14.12 High bandwidth memory architecture. Source: Adapted from Ref. [189].

Compare to HBM1, HBM2 supports up to eight memory dies per stack. The memory size is increased from 2 to 8 Gb per die. The bandwidth is also increased from 125 to 180 Gb/s. All HBM2 are connected to GPU through NVLink2.

14.3 Tensor Processing Unit

Google successfully deployed TPU [191, 192] to support the growing cloud server artificial intelligence demand (search inquiries, machine translation) in 2013. The server employs a large amount of TPUs to support intensive computations. It can perform parallel multiply and add operations to increase the overall throughput. TPU is also evolved from standalone TPU v1 to cloud TPU v2 and v3 configurations [193, 194].

14.3.1 System Architecture

TPU v1 performs the matrix operation using Matrix Multiply Unit (MMU). It consists of a 256×256 Multiplier Accumulator (MAC) unit for eight bits integer multiply and adds. The heart of MAC is derived from the parallel systolic array (Figure 14.13). It is an analogy on how blood rhythmically flows through a biological heart as data transfer from memory to PEs in a rhythmic fashion. All the data is skewed and synchronized by the global clock and feeds into the systolic array for computation.

14.3.2 Brain Floating Point Format

Google also proposes a new 16 bits Brain Floating Point Format (BFP16) [195] to replace 16 bits half-precision IEEE Floating Point Format (FP16) (Figure 14.14). The small mantissa significantly reduces multiplier area and power but achieves the same dynamic range as 32 bits single precision Floating Point Format (FP32), which substantially reduces the memory bandwidth demand without accuracy loss.

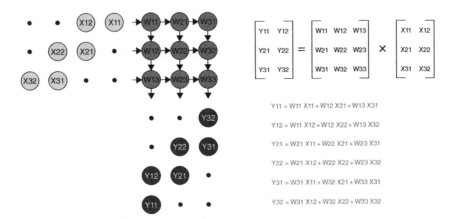

$$\begin{bmatrix} Y11 & Y12 \\ Y21 & Y22 \\ Y31 & Y32 \end{bmatrix} = \begin{bmatrix} W11 & W12 & W13 \\ W21 & W22 & W23 \\ W31 & W32 & W33 \end{bmatrix} \times \begin{bmatrix} X11 & X12 \\ X21 & X22 \\ X31 & X32 \end{bmatrix}$$

Y11 = W11 X11 + W12 X21 + W13 X31

Y12 = W11 X12 + W12 X22 + W13 X32

Y21 = W21 X11 + W22 X21 + W23 X31

Y22 = W21 X12 + W22 X22 + W23 X32

Y31 = W31 X11 + W32 X21 + W33 X31

Y32 = W31 X12 + W32 X22 + W33 X32

Figure 14.13 Systolic array matrix multiplication.

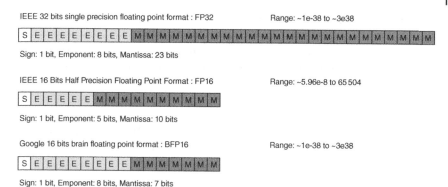

IEEE 32 bits single precision floating point format : FP32   Range: ~1e-38 to ~3e38

Sign: 1 bit, Emponent: 8 bits, Mantissa: 23 bits

IEEE 16 Bits Half Precision Floating Point Format : FP16   Range: ~5.96e-8 to 65 504

Sign: 1 bit, Emponent: 5 bits, Mantissa: 10 bits

Google 16 bits brain floating point format : BFP16   Range: ~1e-38 to ~3e38

Sign: 1 bit, Emponent: 8 bits, Mantissa: 7 bits

Figure 14.14 Brain floating point format. Source: Patterson [195] / Google.

14.3.3 Cloud Configuration

Google extends the standalone TPU v1 to cloud TPU v2 and v3 configurations (Figure 14.15). TPU v2 and v3 pod replace DDR3 memory with high bandwidth memory (HBM). Multiple TPU cores are connected through the dedicated high-speed network to improve overall performance. TPU v2 pod employs 128 v2 cores, TPU v3 pod increases to 256 v3 cores with additional 32Tb memory (Table 14.1).

Figure 14.15 TPU v3 pod configuration. Source: Patterson [195] / UC Regents.

Table 14.1 Tensor processing unit comparison.

Version	TPU v1	TPU v2 pod	TPU v3 pod
Design	2015	2017	2018
Core memory	8Gb DRAM	8Gb HBM	16Gb HBM
Processor element	Single 256 × 256 MAC	Single 128 × 128 MXU	Two 128 × 128 MXU
CPU interface	PCIe 3.0 × 16	PCIe 3.0 × 8	PCIe 3.0 × 8
Performance	92 TOPS	180 TOPS	420 TOPS
Pod cluster	N/A	512 TPU	2048 TPU
Total memory	N/A	4Tb memory	32Tb memory
Application	Inference	Training and inference	Training and inference

14.4 Neural Processing Unit

Due to the surge of data, Edge AI is emerged to address the cloud sever limitations for artificial intelligence applications (i.e., data latency, network bandwidth, and power dissipation). Edge AI is located closed to the data source to offer real-time processing, which reduces the data transfer and resolves the bandwidth bottleneck. Currently, Edge computing is widely used for virtual assistants (Google Home, Amazon Alexa), autonomous vehicles (Tesla), and Internet of Things applications.

14.4.1 System Architecture

Kneron develops the NPU [196, 197] for Edge AI computing (Figures 14.16 and 14.17). It supports image classification and speech recognition applications with popular neural network models, Vgg16, ResNet, GoogleNet, Yolo, LeNet, DenseNet, and MobileNet. Through the model-specific optimization approach, it can achieve 1.5–3x performance improvement. It employs the interleaving architecture to enable parallel convolution and pooling, then replaces the floating-point computation with 8/16 bits fixed-point operations to improve the overall performance. The system also employs deep compression and dynamic memory allocation to improve the overall performance.

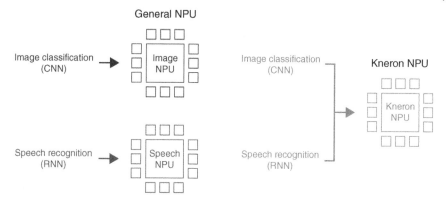

Figure 14.16 System reconfigurability. Source: Adapted from Ward-Foxton [196].

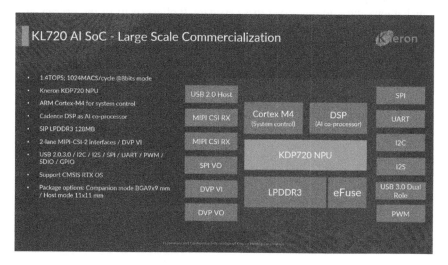

Figure 14.17 Kneron system architecture. Source: Ward-Foxton [196].

14.4.2 Deep Compression

Deep compression technology is applied for both model coefficient and data computation; it prunes the network, eliminates the zero element operations, and achieves over 50% folded compaction ratio. This approach significantly reduces memory usage and high-speed data demand.

14.4.3 Dynamic Memory Allocation

Dynamic memory allocation allows effective resource sharing between the processor cache and system memory; it fully utilizes the memory bandwidth without degrading the overall performance.

The latest Kneron NPU (KL720) achieves 5.8 TOPS at operating frequency 600 MHz. The total power consumption is only 300–500 mW with a 13.7 TOPS/W energy efficiency ratio.

14.4.4 Edge AI Server

Kneron further extends the current Edge AI platform with the smart gateway for traffic safety systems [198] (Figure 14.18), it supports the data transfer between the cloud/edge and edge/edge configurations. It establishes an open platform, which allows the external server to access data. It offers security and privacy protection, all the data is scrambled to hide the sensitive information and the devices are security booted with the blockchain recording all the operations.

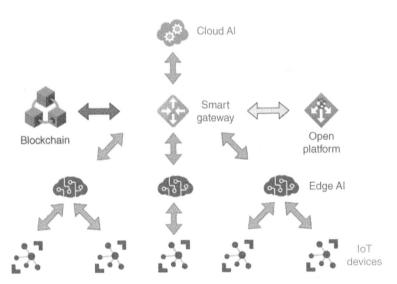

Figure 14.18 Kneron edge AI configuration. Source: Liu et al. [198] / IEEE.

Exercise

1. How does Intel CPU overcome the massively parallel processing challenges?

2. Why is Nvidia "GPU" widely used for neural network training?

3. What is the major drawback of Nvidia GPU?

4. How does Google systolic array speed up the matrix multiplication?

5. Why are the Brain Floating Point Format better than IEEE Floating Point Format?

6. Why are Edge AI systems necessary for deep learning applications?

7. What are the key features of the Kneron NPU?

8. Will Edge AI sever replace cloud one in future?

Appendix A

Kneron Neural Processing Unit

In recent years, the Edge artificial intelligence (AI) computing platform grows rapidly, it connects to the local devices (i.e. sensors) for artificial intelligence of things (AIoT) applications. Edge AI computing platform speeds up the computation with cloud server connection, it reduces the data transfer and improves the overall performance.

Kneron neural processing unit (NPU) – KL520/KL720 (Figure A.1) [199] are excellent Edge AI computing platform, and it supports both image classification and speech recognition with popular neural network models, Vgg16, ResNet, GoogleNet, Yolo, LeNet, DenseNet, and MobileNet. Through the network pruning and model optimization, it improves the overall performance by 1.5–3x. It also quantizes the floating-point number to 8/16 bits fixed point one to further speed up the computation. The system also employs deep compression and dynamic memory allocation to enable the parallel convolution and pooling operations.

Developer Access: http://www.kneron.com/developer_center/

Host Lib Access: https://github.com/kneron/host_lib

Where to Buy: www.kneo.ai or www.kneron.com

Understanding Artificial Intelligence: Fundamentals and Applications, First Edition.
Albert Chun Chen Liu, Oscar Ming Kin Law, and Iain Law.
© 2022 The Institute of Electrical and Electronics Engineers, Inc.
Published 2022 by John Wiley & Sons, Inc.

Figure A.1   Kneron neural processing unit (NPU) [199].

Appendix B

Object Detection – Overview

The Python software platform Keras is chosen for the artificial intelligence programming with TensorFlow backend support. It provides a user-friendly interface with multiple libraries for artificial intelligence implementation. Additional packages are developed to eliminate complex neural network models and allow the users to explore different deep learning applications through Kneron neural processing unit (NPU).

B.1 Kneron Environment Setup

First, it goes to the installation path <install path> to install the Kneron environment using the command git. Git [200] is downloaded from Downloads menu Windows in https://git-scm.com/downloads (Figure B.1). The binary file is called Git-<release>-<64>-bit.exe (i.e. Git-2.29.2.3-64-bit.exe) where <release> is the release name and 64 bits[1] is based on computer architecture.

After the download, click the binary file for installation. It installs the binary in C:\Program Files\Git for 64 bits system (Figure B.2). For another menu, just click the Next button to choose the default options

Then, get Kneron environment and Yolo v3 examples using the commands

```
git clone https://github.com/kneron/host_lib
git clone https://github.com/kneron/kdp_yolov3
```

---

1 The latest tensorflow 2.0 only supports 64 bits computer architecture

Understanding Artificial Intelligence: Fundamentals and Applications, First Edition.
Albert Chun Chen Liu, Oscar Ming Kin Law, and Iain Law.
© 2022 The Institute of Electrical and Electronics Engineers, Inc.
Published 2022 by John Wiley & Sons, Inc.

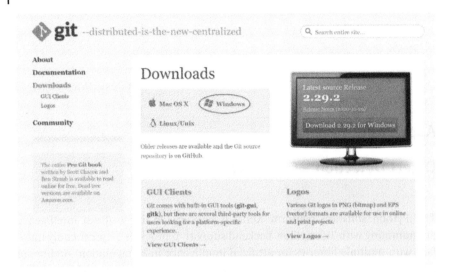

Figure B.1   Git package [200].

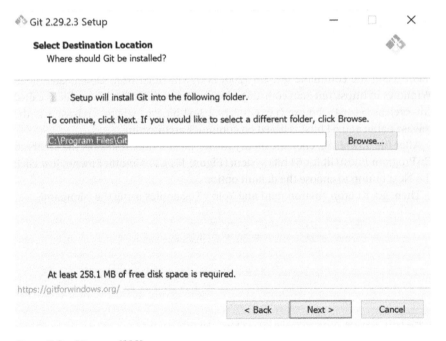

Figure B.2   Git menu [200].

B.2 Python Installation

Since the examples are verified using Python 3.8,[2] please download the latest Python 3.8 package from https://www.python.org (Figures B.3–B.7) [201]. It clicks the **Windows** from the Downloads menu, then selects the executable installer (Windows x86-64 is referred to as 64 bits binary). After the binary file is downloaded, then install the Python package.

To install the Python package, it should choose Customize installation to install the binary in the correct path and select Add Python to PATH option.

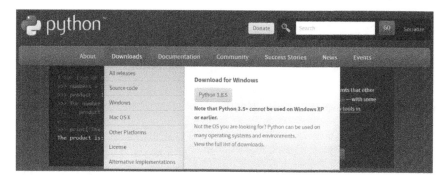

Figure B.3 Python website [201].

- Python 3.8.6 - Sept. 24, 2020
  Note that Python 3.8.6 *cannot* be used on Windows XP or earlier.
  - Download Windows help file
  - Download Windows x86-64 embeddable zip file
  - Download Windows x86-64 executable installer
  - Download Windows x86-64 web-based installer
  - Download Windows x86 embeddable zip file
  - Download Windows x86 executable installer
  - Download Windows x86 web-based installer

Figure B.4 Python package release [201].

---

2 Library packages are not fully compatible with the latest Python 3.9 release.

Figure B.5   Python installation menu [201].

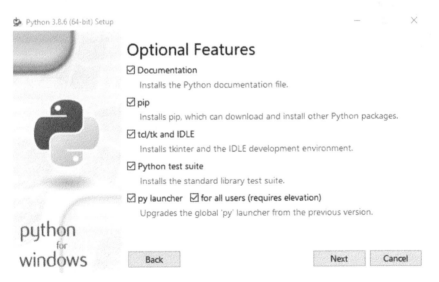

Figure B.6   Python optional features menu [201].

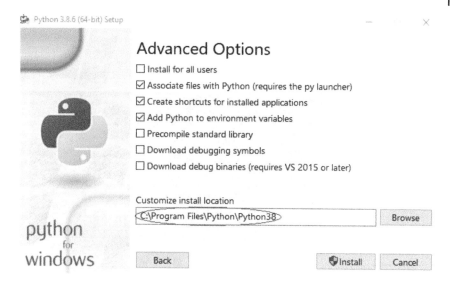

Figure B.7 Python advanced options menu [201].

Select all the Optional Features menu options and specify the install location in the Advanced Options menu. For 64 bits binary, it installs in C:\Program Files\ Python\Python38.

B.3   Library Installation

Window PowerShell (Admin) (Figure B.8) [202] is used for command-line operation; it is invoked from the Start menu

It updates Python Preferred Installer Program (PIP) command

```
python -m pip install -upgrade pip
```

Then, install Kneron NPU distribution wheel files with extension.whl

```
cd <install path>/host_lib/python/packages
pip install .\kdp_host_api-1.0.0_win_-py3-none-any.whl
```

Several library packages are recommended for artificial intelligence applications. TensorFlow is the popular industrial standard for neural processing and acts as the backend support for the Keras framework. opencv and pillow are the image

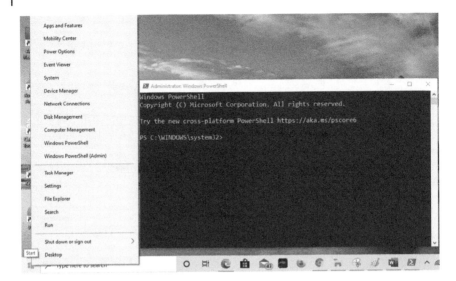

Figure B.8   Windows PowerShell [202].

processing package, matplotlib is the general plotting utility, pygram is a game development platform, which used to program Sony PS3 controller and display the camera captured video for smart drone project. djitellopy controls the DJI Tello drone navigation through software development kit (SDK).

```
pip install keras==2.4.3
pip install tensorflow==2.5.0
pip install opencv-python==4.5.4.58
pip install Pillow==8.1.0
pip install matplotlib==3.4.2
pip install numpy==1.19.5
```

B.4   Driver Installation

Kneron NPU is a unique USB device; it is not currently supported by Microsoft yet. It is required to install a USB driver to initialize Kneron NPU

➢ Download Zadig application from zadig.akeo.ie (Figure B.9) [203]
➢ Connect Kneron NPU to a USB port
➢ Run Zadig application

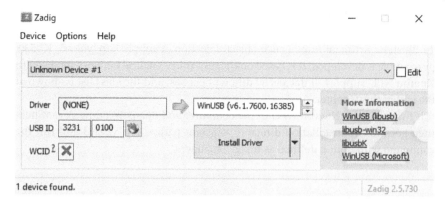

Figure B.9 Driver installation menu [203].

> It detects Kneron NPU as "Unknown Device #1" with USB ID "3231/0100," and the driver file is set to "WinUSB"

B.5 Model Installation

Currently, Kneron offers two NPU releases, KL520 and KL720, and it is required to install the corresponding models for neural processing. It first inserts the NPU into the USB port and invokes the following commands to update the models

For KL520 model installation:

```
cd  <install path>/host_lib
cp ./input_models/KL520/tiny_yolo_v3/*.nef
./app_binaries/KL520/ota/ready_to_load
cp ./app_binaries/KL520/tiny_yolo_v3/*.bin
./app_binaries/KL520/ota/ready_to_load
cd python
python main.py -t KL520-update_app_nef_model
```

For KL720 model installation (optional)

```
cd <install path>/host_lib
cp ./app_binaries/KL720/solution_companion/*.bin
./app_binaries/KL720/dfu/ready_to_load
cd python
python main.py -t KL720-update_fw
```

B.6 Image/Camera Detection

To illustrate artificial intelligence object detection, a simple kdp_yolov3_KL520. py example is developed; it is based on the tiny Yolo v3 neural network model with Kneron NPU support. It detects 80 different classes, and the class list is shown at the end of this Chapter.

It first connects Kneron NPU to the computer and opens Window PowerShell, then goes to the installation directory <instant path>/kdp_yolov3 and run the command with option defined as image or camera

```
python kdp_yolov3_KL520.pl -t <option>
```

The images are stored in <install path>/kdp_yolov3/images subdirectory, and the camera is referred to as the built-in computer webcam.

For image detection (Figure B.10), type the image file name and shows the result in the pop-up window. If the input is empty, it quits the program.

```
python .\kdp_yolov3_KL520.py -t image
Initialize kdp host lib ....

Add kdp device ....
Start kdp host lib ....

Start kdp task: image
Input image file: elephant.jpg
starting ISI mode...

ISI mode succeeded (window = 3)...

image 0 -> 1 object(s)
Input image file:
```

Figure B.10 Image detection [199].

For camera detection (Figure B.11), it shows the frame count and the detection results on the screen. Type "q" in the pop window and quit the program.

```
python .\kdp_yolov3_KL520.py -t camera
Initialize kdp host lib ....

Add kdp device ....
Start kdp host lib ....

Start kdp task: camera
starting ISI mode...

ISI mode succeeded (window = 3)...

image 0 -> 1 object(s)

image 1 -> 1 object(s)

image 2 -> 1 object(s)
```

Figure B.11 Camera detection [199].

B.7 Yolo Class List

```
 1. person
 2. bicycle
 3. car
 4. motorbike
 5. aeroplane
 6. bus
 7. train
 8. truck
 9. boat
10. traffic light
11. fire hydrant
12. stop sign
13. parking meter
14. bench
15. bird
16. cat
17. dog
18. horse
19. sheep
```

20. cow
21. elephant
22. bear
23. zebra
24. giraffe
25. backpack
26. umbrella
27. handbag
28. tie
29. suitcase
30. frisbee
31. skis
32. snowboard
33. sports ball
34. kite
35. baseball bat
36. baseball glove
37. skateboard
38. surfboard
39. tennis racket
40. bottle
41. wine glass
42. cup
43. fork
44. knife
45. spoon
46. bowl
47. banana
48. apple
49. sandwich
50. orange
51. broccoli
52. carrot
53. hot dog
54. pizza
55. donut
56. cake
57. chair
58. sofa
59. potted plant
60. bed
61. dining table
62. toilet
63. tv monitor
64. laptop
65. mouse
66. remote
67. keyboard
68. cell phone
69. microwave
70. oven
71. toaster
72. sink

```
73. refrigerator
74. book
75. clock
76. vase
77. scissors
78. teddy bear
79. hair drier
80. toothbrush
```

Appendix C

Object Detection – Hardware

This laboratory introduces how to apply Kneron neural processing unit (NPU) for object detection. It is required to load the library and define the system parameters, then activate the NPU through several routines with Python 3.8.

C.1 Library Setup

To perform objection detection, several libraries (Figure C.1) are loaded using Python import function. kdp_wrapper is used for object detection and kdp_support supports the examples listed in the book. All the examples are stored in <install path>/kdp_yolov3.

C.2 System Parameters

The system parameters **KDP_UART_DEV** and **KDP_USB_DEV** are used to activate Kneron NPU (Figure C.2). The **user_id** is set to 0 for single-user mode. **ISI_YOLO_ID** is used to define a tiny Yolo v3 neural network model with an image size of 640 x 480.

C.3 NPU Initialization

It first sets up the log file using **init_log**, then initializes host_lib using **lib_init** and adds the Kneron NPU for neural processing with command **connect_usb_device** (Figure C.3).

Understanding Artificial Intelligence: Fundamentals and Applications, First Edition.
Albert Chun Chen Liu, Oscar Ming Kin Law, and Iain Law.
© 2022 The Institute of Electrical and Electronics Engineers, Inc.
Published 2022 by John Wiley & Sons, Inc.

```
1. # Load the system library
2. import argparse
3. import os
4. import ctypes
5. import sys
6. import cv2
7. import time
8. from common import constants, kdp_wrapper,
   kdp_support
```

Figure C.1 Kneron system library [199].

```
1.  # Define KL520 parameters
2.  VENDOR_ID        = 0x3231
3.  KL520_ID         = 0x0100
4.  KL720_ID         = 0x0200
5.  KDP_UART_DEV     = 0
6.  KDP_USB_DEV      = 1
7.  ISI_YOLO_ID      = constants.AppID.APP_TINY_YOLO3
8.  image_source_w   = 640
9.  image_source_h   = 480
10.  image_size       = image_source_w * image_source_h *
    2
11.  loop_count       = 100
12.  user_id          = 0
```

Figure C.2 System parameters [199].

```
1.  # Initialize Kneron USB device
2.  kdp_wrapper.init_log("/tmp/", "mzt.log")
3.  print("Initialize kdp host lib   ....\n")
4.  if (kdp_wrapper.lib_init() < 0):
5.    print("Initialize kdp host lib failure\n")
6.    exit(-1)
7.
8.  # Search USB device
9.  dev_idx = -1
10.  ret, dev_list = kdp_wrapper.scan_usb_devices()
11.
12.  # Add Kneron USB device
13.  print("Add kdp device ....")
14.  for i in range(len(dev_list)):
15.        if (dev_list[i][3] == KL520_ID):
16.             dev_idx =
    kdp_wrapper.connect_usb_device(dev_list[i][0])
17.                 break
18.
19.  if (dev_idx < 0):
20.        print("Add kdp device failure\n")
21.        exit(-1)
22.
23.  # Start Kneron USB device
24.  print("Start kdp host lib ....\n")
25.  if (kdp_wrapper.lib_start() < 0):
26.        print("Start kdp host lib failure")
27.        exit(-1)
```

Figure C.3 NPU initialization source code [199].

C.4   Image Detection

For image detection (Figure C.4), it starts the image streaming inference (ISI) mode for image sequential processing with command **start_isi**, followed by modified **image_inference**, which includes the additional class name for the detected object. Moreover, **frames** are initialized as an empty list to store the image, and the **img_id_tx** is used for statistical analysis.

```
python .\kdp_yolov3.py -t image
Initialize kdp host lib  ....

Add kdp device ....
Start kdp host lib ....

Start kdp task:  image
Input image file: dog.jpg
starting ISI mode...

ISI mode succeeded (window = 3)...

image 0 -> 1 object(s)
Input image file:
```

For latest **host_lib** release, the routine hand_result is used to handle the detection results with **kdp_display_capture_result.** It displays the object class label as well as the bounding box (Figures C.5 and C.6).

```
1.  # Start ISI mode
2.      if kdp_wrapper.start_isi(dev_idx, ISI_YOLO_ID,
    image_source_w, image_source_h):
3.          return -1
4.
5.      # Perform image inference
6.      while image_flag:
7.          image = cv2.imread(image_path)
8.
9.          ret = kdp_support.img_inference(dev_idx,
    ISI_YOLO_ID, image_size, image, img_id_tx, frames,
    handle_result)
10.          if (ret == -1):
11.              break
12.          else:
13.              img_id_tx+=1
```

Figure C.4   Image inference setup source code [199].

```
1.          header_result =
   kdp_wrapper.cast_and_get(inf_res,
   constants.ObjectDetectionRes)
2.          box_result = kdp_wrapper.cast_and_get(
3.              header_result.boxes,
   constants.BoundingBox * header_result.box_count)
4.
5.          boxes = []
6.          for box in box_result:
7.              boxes.append([box.x1, box.y1, box.x2,
   box.y2, box.score, box.class_num])
8.
   kdp_support.kdp_display_capture_result(dev_idx,
   boxes, frames, "yolo")
```

Figure C.5 Object class label and bounding box [199].

Figure C.6 Image detection [199].

```
1.      # Setup webcam capture
2.      capture = kdp_wrapper.setup_capture(0,
   image_source_w, image_source_h)
3.      if capture is None:
4.          return -1
5.
6.      # Start ISI mode
7.      if kdp_wrapper.start_isi(dev_idx, ISI_YOLO_ID,
   image_source_w, image_source_h):
8.          return -1
9.
10.     # Perform video inference
11.     while True:
12.         ret = kdp_wrapper.sync_inference(dev_idx,
   ISI_YOLO_ID, image_size, capture, img_id_tx, frames,
   handle_result)
13.         if (ret == -1):
14.             break
15.         else:
16.             img_id_tx += 1
```

Figure C.7 Camera inference setup source code [199].

C.5 Camera Detection

The difference between the image and camera detection is referred to as the input, and the camera detection captures the image through the computer built-in webcam rather than the file. It captures the image using **setup_capture**, then applies **start_isi** to start ISI mode. It passes the image to the **camera_inference** for object detection. It finally can achieve a frame rate of 6.73 FPS (Figures C.7 and C.8).

```
python .\kdp_yolov3_KL520.py -t camera
Initialize kdp host lib ....

Add kdp device ....
Start kdp host lib ....

Start kdp task: camera
starting ISI mode...

ISI mode succeeded (window = 3)...

image 0 -> 1 object(s)

image 1 -> 1 object(s)
```

Figure C.8 Camera detection [199].

Appendix D

Hardware Transfer Mode

For Kneron neural processing unit (NPU), it schedules the task in three transfer modes, serial, pipeline and parallel. An example, **kdp_yolov3_mode_KL520**, is developed to demonstrate the performance improvement with the three options, serial, pipeline, and parallel using Python 3.8. Please launch kdp_yolov3_mode. py in <install path>/kdp_yolov3

```
python .\kdp_yolov3_mode_KL520.py -t <option>
```

D.1   Serial Transfer Mode

For serial transfer (Figures D.1 and D.2), it is the same as the example **kdp_yolov3_KL520** shown in Chapter 3. It first initializes Kneron NPU and starts in image streaming inference (ISI) mode, then, it captures the video from the built-in camera and transfers the frame to Kneron NPU for object detection using **sync_inference**.

The frame is transferred to Kneron NPU in serial order, then performs the object detection using the Kneron inference engine. After the object recognition is completed, the result is returned to the host computer. The frame rate is 6.73FPS.

Understanding Artificial Intelligence: Fundamentals and Applications, First Edition.
Albert Chun Chen Liu, Oscar Ming Kin Law, and Iain Law.
© 2022 The Institute of Electrical and Electronics Engineers, Inc.
Published 2022 by John Wiley & Sons, Inc.

```
python .\kdp_yolov3_mode_KL520.py -t serial
Initialize kdp host lib  ....

Add kdp device ....
Start kdp host lib ....

Start kdp task:  serial
starting ISI mode...

ISI mode succeeded (window = 3)...

image 0 -> 1 object(s)

image 1 -> 1 object(s)
```

```
1.      # Start ISI mode.
2.    if kdp_wrapper.start_isi(dev_idx, ISI_YOLO_ID,
   image_source_w, image_source_h):
3.          exit(-1)
4.
5.    img_id_tx  = 0
6.    start_time = time.time()
7.    while (img_id_tx < loop_count):
8.          ret = kdp_wrapper.sync_inference(dev_idx,
   ISI_YOLO_ID, image_size, capture, img_id_tx, frames,
   handle_result)
9.
10.              if (ret == -1):
11.                  break
12.          else:
13.                  img_id_tx += 1
```

Figure D.1   Serial transfer source code [199].

Figure D.2   Serial transfer operation [199].

D.2   Pipeline Transfer Mode

For pipeline transfer (Figures D.3 and D.4), it starts Kneron NPU in ISI mode, then fills up the buffer using **fill_buffer**. Kneron NPU fetches the captured frame from the buffer and transfers the data to the Kneron inference engine for object recognition through pipeline inference. Since the frame is stored in the buffer, it reduces the frame capture waiting time. It significantly improves the overall performance by 56%, and the frame rate is increased to 10.52FPS.

```
python .\kdp_yolov3_mode.py -t pipeline
Initialize kdp host lib  ....

Add kdp device ....
Start kdp host lib ....

Start kdp task:  pipeline
starting ISI mode...

ISI mode succeeded (window = 3)...

starting ISI inference ...

image 1234 -> 1 object(s)

image 1235 -> 1 object(s)
```

D.3   Parallel Transfer Mode

For parallel transfer (Figures D.5 and D.6), it enables Kneron NPU in parallel transfer using **start_isi_parallel**, then it fills up the buffer using the same routine **fill_buffer**. Kneron NPU transfers the data from the buffer to the Kneron inference engine for object detection with **pipe_inference**. The parallel transfer further improves the performance by 85.98% and achieves the frame rate of 12.52FPS.

```
1.  # Start ISI mode.
2.    if kdp_wrapper.start_isi(dev_idx, ISI_YOLO_ID,
    image_source_w, image_source_h):
3.            exit(-1)
4.
5.    start_time = time.time()
6.      # Fill up the image buffers.
7.    ret, img_id_tx, img_left, buffer_depth =
    kdp_wrapper.isi_fill_buffer(dev_idx, capture,
    image_size, frames)
8.    if ret:
9.            exit(-1)
10.
11.  # Send the rest and get result in loop, with 2
    images alternatively
12.          print("Companion image buffer depth = ",
    buffer_depth)
13.          kdp_wrapper.isi_pipeline_inference(
14.            dev_idx, ISI_YOLO_ID, loop_count -
    buffer_depth, image_size,
15.            capture, img_id_tx, img_left, buffer_depth,
    frames, handle_result)
```

Figure D.3   Pipeline transfer source code [199].

Figure D.4 Pipeline transfer operation [199].

```
1.          # Start ISI mode.
2.    if kdp_wrapper.start_isi_parallel_ext(dev_idx,
      ISI_YOLO_ID, image_source_w, image_source_h):
3.          exit(-1)
4.
5.    start_time = time.time()
6.      # Fill up the image buffers.
7.    ret, img_id_tx, img_left, buffer_depth =
      kdp_wrapper.isi_fill_buffer(dev_idx, capture,
      image_size, frames)
8.    if ret:
9.          exit(-1)
10.
11.     # Send the rest and get result in loop, with 2
      images alternatively
12.         print("Companion image buffer depth = ",
      buffer_depth)
13.         kdp_wrapper.isi_pipeline_inference(
14.         dev_idx, ISI_YOLO_ID, loop_count -
      buffer_depth, image_size,
15.         capture, img_id_tx, img_left, buffer_depth,
      frames, handle_result)
```

Figure D.5 Parallel transfer source code [199].

Figure D.6 Parallel transfer operation [199].

```
python .\kdp_yolov3_mode_KL520.py -t parallel
Initialize kdp host lib ....

Add kdp device ....
Start kdp host lib ....

Start kdp task: parallel
starting ISI mode...

ISI mode succeeded (window = 3)...

starting ISI inference ...

Companion image buffer depth = 3
image 1234 -> 0 object(s)

image 1235 -> 0 object(s)
```

Due to Kneron hardware/software integration, it significantly improves Yolo v3 object detection performance using different transfer modes. The performance comparison is summarized in Table D.1.

Table D.1 Tiny Yolo v3 performance comparison.

Mode	Runtime (s)	Frame rate (FPS)
Serial	0.1486	6.73
Pipeline	0.0951	10.52
Parallel	0.0799	12.52

Appendix E

Object Detection – Software (Optional)

This laboratory introduces the latest Yolo v5 release for object detection; it provides faster training with a smaller neural network model. The Yolo v5 is implemented using Pytorch with Nvidia CUDA[1], and Microsoft Visual C++[2] languages. Since some computer system does not support Nvidia GPU, the laboratory is optional

E.1   Library Setup

It first installs the Pytorch from the website www.pytorch.org (Figure E.1) [204], then goes to the menu "Get Started." It automatically detects the system configuration and shows the installation information, including the release version, operating system, language, computes platform, and installation command:

   Then, execute the installation commands:

```
pip install torch==1.8.0+cu102 torchvision==0.9.0+cu102 torchaudio===0.8.0
-f https://download.pytorch.org/whl/torch_stable.html
```

   From the installation command, the keyword, cu102, is referred to as CUDA language release. It is varied for different system configurations.

---

1 Nvidia CUDA language is machine dependent, the readers should visit Nvidia website to access the installation instructions.

2 Microsoft Visual C++ language is used to support the PyTorch compilation, the readers should visit Microsoft website to access the latest release.

Understanding Artificial Intelligence: Fundamentals and Applications, First Edition.
Albert Chun Chen Liu, Oscar Ming Kin Law, and Iain Law.
© 2022 The Institute of Electrical and Electronics Engineers, Inc.
Published 2022 by John Wiley & Sons, Inc.

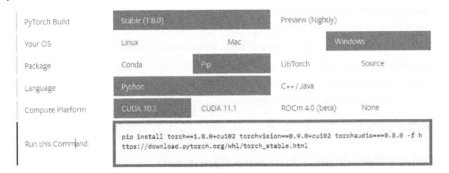

Figure E.1 PyTorch installation menu [204].

After that, it installs Yolo v5 release with the commands

```
git clone https://github.com/ultralytics/yolov5
pip install -r requirements.txt
```

Yolo v5 [205] supports different models (Figure E.2), yolov5s (14.5 Mb), yolov5m (42.1 Mb), yolov5l (92.3 Mb), yolov5x (172.0 Mb) with Average Precision (COCO AP). The model with a higher COCO AP score offers more accurate object detections.

yolov5 can performs the object detection using webcam, photos, and videos with following commands:

```
python detect.py --source 0                    # webcam
python detect.py --source <path>/<image>.jpg # image
python detect.py --source <path>/<video>.mp4 # video
```

It can be changed to a different Yolo v5 model using the switch --weight <model>

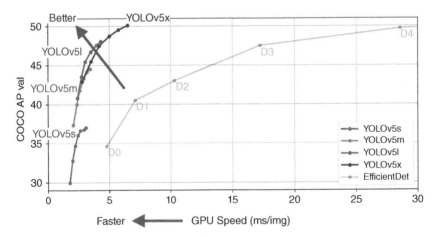

Figure E.2 yolov5 object detection [205].

E.2   Image Detection

To perform the image detection (Figure E.3), it invokes the command **detect.py** and specifies the image full path **<path>/<image>.jpg** with option **--source**

```
python .\detect.py --source data\images\bus.jpg
Namespace(agnostic_nms=False, augment=False, classes=None, conf_thres=0.25,
device='', exist_ok=False, img_size=640, iou_thres=0.45, name='exp',
project='runs/detect', save_conf=False, save_txt=False,
source='data\\images\\bus.jpg', update=False, view_img=False,
weights='yolov5s.pt')
YOLOv5 v4.0-41-g9a3da79 torch 1.7.0+cu110 CUDA:0 (GeForce RTX 2060,
6144.0MB)

Fusing layers...
Model Summary: 224 layers, 7266973 parameters, 0 gradients, 17.0 GFLOPS
image 1/1
C:\Users\oscar\OneDrive\Personal\Github\yolov5\data\images\bus.jpg: 640x480
4 persons, 1 bus, Done. (0.060s)
Results saved to runs\detect\exp5
Done. (0.212s)
```

Figure E.3   Image detection [205].

The results are stored in the subdirectory runs\detect shown by the last statement, **Results saved to runs\detect\exp5**

E.3   Video Detection

Similarly, it performs the video detection (Figure E.4) using the same command, **detect.py** with video full path using the option **--source <path>/<video>.mp4**. The software automatically identifies the file type and perform video detection

```
python .\detect.py --source data\images\hong_kong_traffic.mp4
Namespace(agnostic_nms=False, augment=False, classes=None, conf_thres=0.25,
device='', exist_ok=False, img_size=640, iou_thres=0.45, name='exp',
project='runs/detect', save_conf=False, save_txt=False,
source='data\\images\\hong_kong_traffic.mp4', update=False, view_img=False,
weights='yolov5s.pt')
YOLOv5 v4.0-41-g9a3da79 torch 1.7.0+cu110 CUDA:0 (GeForce RTX 2060,
6144.0MB)

Fusing layers...
Model Summary: 224 layers, 7266973 parameters, 0 gradients, 17.0 GFLOPS
video 1/1 (1/633)
C:\Users\oscar\OneDrive\Personal\Github\yolov5\data\images\hong_kong_traffi
c.mp4: 384x640 2 persons, 4 cars, 2 buss, 1 traffic light, Done. (0.072s)


.......

video 1/1 (633/633)
C:\Users\oscar\OneDrive\Personal\Github\yolov5\data\images\hong_kong_traffi
c.mp4: 384x640 2 cars, 1 bus, 2 trucks, Done. (0.012s)
Results saved to runs\detect\exp6
Done. (16.278s)
```

Figure E.4   Video detection [205].

The results are also stored in the subdirectory runs\detect specified by the statement, **Results saved to runs\detect\exp6**

References

[1] Schwab, K. (2016). The Fourth Industrial Revolution: what it means, how to respond. *World Economic Forum.*

[2] Hatzakis, E.D. (2016). The Fourth Industrial Revolution. Ban of America Merrill Lynch.

[3] (2019). The Evolution of Industry 1.0 to 4.0. Seekmoment [Online].

[4] Krizhevsky, A., Sutskever, I., and Hinton, G.E. (2012). ImageNet classification with deep convolutional neural network. *Advances in Neural Information Processing Systems 25,* pp. 1–9.

[5] Strachnyi, K. (2019). Brief History of Neural Network (23 January) [Online].

[6] McCulloch, W.S. and Pitts, W.H. (1943). A logical calculus of the ideas immanent in nervous activity. *The Bulletin of Mathematical Biophysics* 5 (4): 115–133.

[7] Rosenblatt, F. (1958). The perceptron – a probabilistic model for information storage and organization in the Brain. *Psychological Review* 65 (6): 386–408.

[8] Minsky, M.L. and Papert, S.A. (1969). Perceptrons.

[9] Hopfield, J.J. (1982). Neural networks and physical systems with emergent collective computational abilities. *Proceeding of National Academy of Sciences* 79: 2554–2558.

[10] Lecun, Y., Bottou, L., and Haffnrt, P. (1998). Gradient-based learning applied to document recognition. *Proceedings of the IEEE* 86 (11): 2278–2324.

[11] Russakobsky, O., Deng, J., Su, H. et al. (2015). ImageNet large scale visual recognition challenge. arXiv:1409.0575v3.

[12] Howard, A.G. (2013). Some improvements on deep convolutional neural network based image classification. arXiv:1312.5402v1.

[13] Simonyan, K. and Zisserman, A. (2014). Very deep convolutional networks for large-scale image recognition. arXiv: 14091556v6.

Understanding Artificial Intelligence: Fundamentals and Applications, First Edition.
Albert Chun Chen Liu, Oscar Ming Kin Law, and Iain Law.
© 2022 The Institute of Electrical and Electronics Engineers, Inc.
Published 2022 by John Wiley & Sons, Inc.

[14] Szegedy, C., Liu, W., Jia, Y. et al. (2015). Going Deeper with Convolutions. In *IEEE Conference on Computer Vision and Pattern Recognition (CVPR)*, Boston, MA (7–12 June 2015).

[15] He, K., Zhang, X., Ren, S., and Sun, J. (2016). Deep residual learning for image recognition. In *IEEE Conference on Computer Vision and Pattern Recognition (CVPR)*, Las Vegas, NV (27–30 June 2016).

[16] Liu, A.C.C. and Law, O.M.K. (2021). *Artificial Intelligence Hardware: Challenges and Solutions*. Wiley.

[17] Zeiler, M.D. and Fergus, R. (2013). Visualizing and Understanding Convolutional Networks. arVix: 1311.2901v3.

[18] Sharma, P. (2019). Image classification vs. object detection vs. image segmentation. Medium (20 August) [Online].

[19] (2020). Object detection vs. object recognition vs. image segmentation. GeeksforGeeks (27 February) [Online].

[20] Li, F.-F., Justin, J., and Serena, Y. (2018). Lecture 11: dection and segmentation (Stanford CS231 Lecture Note) (10 May) [Online].

[21] Senaar, K. (2019). Facial recognition applications – security, retail, and beyond. *Emerj* (22 November) [Online].

[22] de Jesus, A. (2019). Artificial intelligence in video marketing – emotion recognition, video generation, and more. *Emerj* (15 February) [Online].

[23] de Jesus, A. (2019). Artificial intelligence in gestural interfaces – possible near-term applications. *Emerj* (21 November) [Online].

[24] Roth, M. (2019). Computer vision in healthcare – current applications. *Emerj* (5 August) [Online].

[25] Bishop, T. (2018). Amazon Go is finally a go: sensor-infused store opens to the public Monday, with no checkout lines. GeekWire (21 January) [Online].

[26] Abadicio, M. (2019),.Facial recognition at airports – current applications. *Emerj* (22 November) [Online].

[27] Madhavan, R. (2019). Natural language processing – current applications and future possibilities. *Emerj* (13 December) [Online].

[28] Elvis (2018). Deep learning for NLP: an overview of recent trends. Medium (23 August) [Online].

[29] Modern deep learning techniques applied to natural language processing. NLPoverview [Online].

[30] Christopher Olah (2015). Understanding LSTM networks. Colah's blog (27 August) [Online].

[31] de Jesus, A. (2019). Artificial intelligence for customer service – current and future applications. *Emerj* (22 November) [Online].

[32] Mejia, N. (2020). Artificial intelligence at UBS – current applications and initiatives. *Emerj* (15 April) [Online].

[33] de Jesus, A. (2019). AI for speech recognition – current companies, technology, and trends, *Emerj* (16 February) [Online].

[34] Madhavan, R. (2019). Machine translation – 14 current applications and services. *Emerj* (22 November) [Online].

[35] Machine translation. Microsoft [Online].

[36] Sennaar, K. (2019). AI for virtual medical assistants – 4 current applications. *Emerj* [Online].

[37] Faggella, D. (2019). AI for voice transcription – comparing upcoming startups and established players. *Emerj* (20 May) [Online].

[38] de Jesus, A. (2019). AI for self-driving car safety – current applications. *Emerj* (16 January) [Online].

[39] Madhavan, R. (2019). How self-driving cars work – a simple overview. *Emerj* (3 June) [Online].

[40] Stayton, E. and Stilgoe, J. (2020). It's time to rethink levels of automation for self-driving vehicles. *IEEE Technology and Society Magazine* 39 (3): 13–19.

[41] What is an autonomous car? Synopsys [Online].

[42] Law, W. (2019). An introduction to autonomous vehicles. *TowardsDataScience* (11 September) [Online].

[43] Bayyou, D.G. (2019). Artificially intelligent self-driving vehicle technologies benefits and challenges. *International Journal of Emerging Technology in Computer Science and Electronics* 26 (3): 5–13.

[44] Buller, W. Benchmarking sensors for vehicle computer vision systems. *Michigan Tech* [Online].

[45] Burke, K. (2019). How does a self-driving car see?. Nvidia (15 April) [Online].

[46] Faggella, D. (2020). Computer vision applications: shopping, driving and more. *Emerj* (14 March) [Online].

[47] Dwivedi, P. (2017). Tracking a self-driving car with high precision. TowardsDataScience (30 April) [Online].

[48] Dwivedi, P. (2017). Planning the path for a self-driving car on a highway. TowardsDataScience (9 August) [Online].

[49] Podfeet (2019). Tesla tech – so many levels of self driving. *PodFeet* (15 August) [Online].

[50] Koon, J. (2019). Will vehicle-to-vehicle communication ever take off? Engineering (19 February) [Online].

[51] What is vehicle to infrastructure V2I technology? rgbsi [Online].

[52] (2017). Vehicle to pedestrian communication technology. Pansonic [Online].

[53] Walker, J. (2019). Autonomous vehicle regulations – near-term challenges and consequences. *Emerj* (3 February) [Online].

[54] (2019). Federal Automated Vehicles Policy. U.S. Department of Transportation [Online].

[55] (2018). Introduction to Drones – A Drone Guide for Dummies! Airbuzz (2 September) [Online].

[56] French, S. (2018). What does the inside of a drone look like_ Here's a dissection of a DJI Phantom – the drone girl. Drone Girl (26 March) [Online].

[57] Walker, J. (2019). Industrial uses of drones – 5 current business applications. *Emerj* (30 January) [Online].

[58] Higgins, A. How to deploy drones for construction management, even if you're a complete beginner. Autodesk [Online].

[59] de Jesus, A. (2019). Drones for agriculture – current applications. *Emerj* (2 January) [Online].

[60] Drones for search & rescue missions. AltiGator [Online].

[61] Vaniukov, S. (2020). How AI in healthcare is changing the industry. Data Science Central (25 February) [Online].

[62] Jameel, F. (2019). AI in healthcare – a quiet revolution about to get loud. Abdul Latif Jameel (28 October) [Online].

[63] Tahmasssebi, N. (2018). Artificial intelligence in healthcare. PlugandPlay (23 August) [Online].

[64] Steedman, M., Taylor, K., Properzi, F. et al. (2019). Intelligent biopharma: forging the links across the value chain. Deloitte Centre for Health Solutions.

[65] Faggella, D. (2019). Artificial intelligence in Telemedicine and Telhealth – 4 current applications. *Emerj* (16 February) [Online].

[66] AI provides doctors with diagnostic advice: how will AI change? Fujitsu (29 November) [Online].

[67] Marr, B. (2018). How is AI used in healthcare – 5 powerful real-world examples that show the latest advances. Forbes [Online].

[68] 6 benefits of implementing robotic process automation (RPA) in healthcare. Medium, 26 September 2019 [Online].

[69] Hale, C. (2020). GE Healthcare rolls out new AI-powered chest X-ray suite. MedTech (19 June) [Online].

[70] Akkus, Z., Galimzianova, A., Hoogi, A. et al. (2017). Deep Learning for Brain MRI Segmentation: State of the Art and Future Directions. Spring Link.

[71] Shaikh, N. (2017). Implementing AI in wearable health apps for better tomorrow. Dzone (22 July) [Online].

[72] The AI industry series – top healthcare AI trends to watch. CBInsights [Online].

[73] Jordan, R. (2020). Unlocking the potential of electronic health records with AI. RTInsights (31 January) [Online].

[74] Bharadwaj, R. (2019). Artificial intelligence for medical billing and coding. *Emerj* (22 November) [Online].

[75] Alamanou, M.T. (2019). AI drug discovery: top investors and top startups. Medium (3 October) [Online].

[76] Sennaar, K. (2019). AI and machine learning for clinical trials – examining 3 current applications. *Emerj* (5 March) [Online].

[77] Mejia, N. (2019). Artificial intelligence for clinical trials in pharma – current applications. *Emerj* (30 April) [Online].

[78] Mejia, N. (2019). Artificial intelligence in medical robotics – current applications and possibilities. *Emerj* (29 April) [Online].

[79] (2019). Robotics surgery: the role of AI and collaborative. Robotic Online Marketing Team (9 July) [Online].

[80] Bharadwaj, R. (2019). Applications of artificial intelligence in elderly care robotics. *Emerj* (10 February) [Online].

[81] Ilchenko, V. (2020). AI Adoption in healthcare:10 Pros and Cons. ByteAnt (7 September) [Online].

[82] Koteshov, D. (2019). The State of AI in banking and financial. EliNext (18 January) [Online].

[83] Phaneuf, A. (2020). Artificial intelligence in financial services: applications and benefits of AI in finance. Business Insider (9 September) [Online].

[84] (2019). AI helps businesses get smarter about fraud. Pymnts (13 June) [Online].

[85] Mejia, N. (2019). Artificial intelligence at mastercard – current projects and services. *Emerj* (14 March) [Online].

[86] Mejia, N. (2019). Artificial intelligence for credit card companies – current applications. *Emerj* (29 May) [Online].

[87] de Jesus, A. (2019). Machine learning for credit card fraud – 7 applications for detection and prevention, *Emerj* (22 November) [Online].

[88] Neevista Pty Ltd (2019). How machine learning can transform the financial forecasting process. Medium (11 December) [Online].

[89] Seeing the future more clearly: how machine learning can transform the financial forecasting process. protiviti [Online].

[90] Amazon Forecast. Amazon [Online].

[91] Knowlab (2019). How is Machine Learning Used in Stock Market? Knowlab (20 May) [Online].

[92] Webmaster (2013). Artificial intelligence: the future of stock market trading. kscripts (12 December) [Online].

[93] Voigt, A. Artificial intelligence stock trading software: top 5. Daytradingz [Online].

[94] Bharadwaj, R. (2019). Stock brokerage firms and artificial intelligence – current applications. *Emerj* (16 February) [Online].

[95] Coinspectator (2018). AI in finance: from science fiction to modern. CoinSpectator (4 November) [Online].

[96] Sloane, T. (2018). The 18 top use cases of artificial intelligence in banks. Payments Journal (6 November) [Online].

[97] Faggella, D. (2020). AI in banking – an analysis of America's 7 top banks. *Emerj* (14 March) [Online].

[98] Mejia, N. (2019). Machine vision in banking – facial recognition and OCR. *Emerj* (23 January) [Online].

[99] Narang, A. (2018). How artificial intelligence is impacting the accounting profession. SmallBusinessBonfire, (1 May) [Online].

[100] Rana, R. (2020), How artificial intelligence will impact the accounting industry? Ace Cloud Hosting (24 January) [Online].

[101] Chad Brooks (2020). How AI and automation technology can help accountants. Business.com [Online].

[102] Nagarajah, E. (2016). What does automation mean for the accouting profession? *Accountant Today*.

[103] Faggella, D. (2020). AI in the accounting big four – comparing deloitte, PwC, KPMG and EY. *Emerj* (3 April) [Online].

[104] Mejia, N. (2019). Machine vision in insurance – current applications. *Emerj* (13 December) [Online].

[105] Bharadwaj, R. (2020). What do insurance experts think about AI in claims processing? *Emerj* (27 January) [Online].

[106] Bharadwaj, R. (2019). Machine vision in finance – current applications and trends. *Emerj* (7 October) [Online].

[107] Prakash, A. (2019). Role of artificial intelligence in retail industry. Appventurez (16 October) [Online].

[108] Makhija, R. (2019). Artificial intelligence in ecommerce. Guru TechnoLabs [Online].

[109] Dominic, B. (2019). 8 innovative ways to amalgamate artificial intelligence (AI) with E-commerce! *Cogneesol* 6: 12.

[110] Bharadwaj, R. (2020). Business intelligence in retail – current applications. *Emerj* 11: 3.

[111] Faggella, D. (2019). Crowdsourced search relevance for eCommerce and online retail. *Emerj* (15 February) [Online].

[112] de Jesus, A. (2020). Augmented reality shopping and artificial intelligence – near-term applications. *Emerj* (20 April) [Online].

[113] de Jesus, A. (2019). Virtual mirrors and computer vision – 9 current applications. *Emerj* (22 November) [Online].

[114] de Jesus, A. (2019). Virtual reality shopping and artificial intelligence – 5 near-term applications. *Emerj* (22 November) [Online].

[115] Bharadwaj, R. (2019). Artificial intelligence for high frequency retail – pricing, inventory and margins optimization. *Emerj* (15 February) [Online].

[116] Wycislik-Wilson, M. (2018). Amazon Go, the AI-powered, checkout-free. *Betanews* (22 January) [Online].

[117] Tillman, M. (2020). What is Amazon Go, where is it, and how does it work? Pocket-lint (25 February) [Online].

[118] Cheng, A. (2019). Why Amazon Go may soon change the way we shop? Poctet-lint (13 January) [Online].

[119] Faggella, D. (2020). Artificial intelligence in retail – 10 present and future use cases. *Emerj* (4 March) [Online].

[120] Ackerman, E. (2018). Brad Porter, VP of robotics at Amazon, on warehouse automation, machine learning, and his first robot. IEEE Spectrum (27 September) [Online].

[121] Lee, A. (2017). Automated warehousing systems at Amazon. Harvard Business School (12 November) [Online].

[122] Pierce, D. (2013). Delivery drones are coming: Jeff Bezos promises half-hour shipping with Amazon Prime Air. Theverge.com (1 December) [Online].

[123] Walker, J. (2019). Inventory management with machine learning – 3 use cases in industry. *Emerj* (20 May) [Online].

[124] Al, R. (2018). Artificial intelligence for inventory management. Medium (3 July) [Online].

[125] Mejia, N. (2020). Machine vision in retail – current use-cases and applications. *Emerj* (23 March) [Online].

[126] Jennifer (2019). How is AI transforming supply chain management. *Mnubo* (30 August) [Online].

[127] Columbus, L. (2018).10 ways machine learning is revolutionizing supply chain management. *Forbes* (11 January) [Online].

[128] Usmsys (2020). 10+ AI use cases/applications in manufacturing industry 2020. *Usmsys* (22 May) [Online].

[129] Columbus, L. (2019). 10 ways machine learning is revolutionizing manufacturing in 2019. *Emerj* (11 August) [Online].

[130] Columbus, L. (2020). 10 ways AI is improving manufacture In 2020. *Forbes* (18 May) [Online].

[131] Renner, L.A. (2020). How can artificial intelligence be applied in manufacturing? Medium (3 March) [Online].

[132] Crockett, M. (2020). Different ways industrial AI is revolutionizing manufacturing. Manufacturing Tomorrow (24 January) [Online].

[133] Polachowska, K. (2019). 10 use cases of AI in manufacturing. Neoteric (27 June) [Online].

[134] Roman Chuprina (2020). AI and machine learning in manufacturing: the complete guide. SPD Group (22 January) [Online].

[135] Walker, J. (2019). Machine learning in manufacturing – present and future use-cases. *Emerj* (23 October) [Online].

[136] (2018). 7 ways artificial intelligence is positively impacting manufacturing. AMFG (10 August) [Online].

[137] (2019). Future factory: how technology is transforming manufacturing. CBInsights (17 June) [Online].

[138] (2019). Toward future farming: how artificial intelligence is transforming agriculture industry. Wipro [Online].

[139] Artificial intelligence in agriculture: 6 smart ways to improve the industry and gain profit. IDAP [Online].

[140] Faggella, D. (2020). AI in agriculture – present applications and impact. *Emerj* (18 May) [Online].

[141] Sennaaar, K. (2019). Agricultural robots – present and future applications (Videos Included). *Emerj* (3 February) [Online].

[142] Gossett, S. (2019). Farming & agriculture robots. Built-in (30 July) [Online].

[143] Sheikh, K. (2020). A Growing Presence on the Farm: Robots. *The New York Times* (13 February) [Online].

[144] Bisen, V.S. (2019). How AI can help in agriculture: five applications and use cases. Vsinghbisen (25 June) [Online].

[145] Potter, W. (2020). AI can tackle the climate emergency – if developed. Shutterstock (23 April) [Online].

[146] RV Studios for Microsoft (2019). AI enables the future of farming. *cnet* (13 December) [Online].

[147] Buttice, C. (2020). Top 14 AI use cases: artificial intelligence in smart cities. AltaML (27 March) [Online].

[148] Tan, A. (2020). Opportunities for greater use of AI in smart cities. *FutureIoT* (18 March) [Online].

[149] Shea, S. and Burns, E. (2020). Smart city. TechTarget [Online].

[150] Smart cities: acceleration, technology, cases and evolutions in the smart city. I-Scoop [Online].

[151] Smart Taipei Brochure. City of Taipei Government [Online].

[152] (2020). Smart ciiy Index 2020. IMD.

[153] P. Publishing (2019). Artificial intelligence for smart cities. Becoming Human (9 August) [Online].

[154] Mishra, G. (2019). AI in smart cities: making all the difference in the world. Cyfuture (9 May) [Online].

[155] Walker, J. (2019). Smart city artificial intelligence applications and trends. *Emerj* (31 January) [Online].

[156] Miramant, J. (2020). AI and IoT: transportation management in smart cities. Unite.ai (28 August) [Online].

[157] Bisen, V.S. (2020). How AI can be used in smart cities: applications role & challenge. Medium, [Online].

[158] Wolfe, F. (2017). How artificial intelligence will revolutionize the energy industry. Harvard University (28 August) [Online].

[159] de Leon, S.P. (2019). The role of smart grids and AI in the race to zero emissions. Forbes (20 March) [Online].

[160] What are smart cities? *CBInsights* (15 December 2020) [Online].

[161] Woetzel, J., Remes, J., Boland, B. et al. (2018). Smart cities: digital solutions for a more. McKinsey Global Institute (6 May) [Online].

[162] Eggers, W.D., Schatsky, D., and Viechnicki, P. (2017). AI-augmented government – using cognitive technologies to redesign the public sector work. Deloitte University Press.

[163] Eggers, W.D. and Beyer, T. (2019). AI-augmented government climbing the AI maturity curve. Deloitte Insights (24 June) [Online].

[164] Campbell, T.A. and Fetzer, J. (2019). Artifical intelligence: state initiatives and C-suite implications. *Emerj* (30 August) [Online].

[165] Price, M., Eggers, W.D., and Sen, R. (2018). Smart government: unleashing the power of data. Deloitte Insights (7 February) [Online].

[166] Ciarniello, A. (2020). Artificial intelligence and national security: integrating online data. *Security Magazine* (21 Octobor) [Online].

[167] Faggella, D. (2019). Artificial intelligence and security: current applications and tomorrow's potentials. *Emerj* (20 May) [Online].

[168] Ramachandran, K. (2019). Cybersecurity issues in the AI world. Deloitte Insights (11 September) [Online].

[169] Eggers, W.D., Fishman, T., and Kishnani, P. (2019), AI-augmented human services. Deloitte Insights [Online].

[170] Fishman, T. and Eggers, W. (2019). AI-augmented human services – using cognitive technologies to transform program delivery. Deloitte Insights (31 October) [Online].

[171] Eggers, W.D., Schatsky, D., and Viechnicki, P. (2017). AI-augmented government – using cognitive technologies to redesign public sector work. Deloitte Insights (26 April) [Online].

[172] Viechnicki, P. and Eggers, W.D. (2017). How much time and money can AI save government? Deloitte Insights (26 April) [Online].

[173] Faggella, D. (2019). AI and machine vision for law enforcement – use-cases and policy implications. *Emerj* (20 May) [Online].

[174] Bump, P. (2018). Facial recognition in law enforcement – 6 current applications. *Emerj* (29 November) [Online].

[175] Faggella, D. (2019). AI for crime prevention and detection – 5 current applications. *Emerj* (2 February) [Online].

[176] Joshi, N. (2020). The rise of AI in crime prevention and detection. *BBN Times* (1 Octobor) [Online].

[177] Abadicio, M. (2019). AI at the US Department of Homeland Security – Current Projects. *Emerj* (16 April) [Online].

[178] The Law Library of Congress, Global Legal Research Directorate (2019). Regulation of artificial intelligence in selected jurisdictions. The Law Library of Congress.

[179] Walch, K. (2020). AI laws are coming. Forbes (20 February) [Online].

[180] Callahan, G. (2020). Artificial intelligence law: how the law applies to AI. Rev (13 November) [Online].

[181] Dalmia, N. and Schatsky, D. (2019). The rise of data and AI ethics. Deloitte Insights (24 June) [Online].

[182] Schatsky, D., Katyal, V., Iyengar, S., and Chauhan, R. (2019). Can AI be ethical? Deloitte Insights (17 April) [Online].

[183] Carrasco, M., Mills, S., Whybrew, A., and Jura, A. (2019). The citizen's perspective on the use of AI in government. BCG (1 March) [Online].

[184] You, Y., Zhang, Z., Hsieh, C.-J. et al. (2018). ImageNet training in minutes. arXiv:1709.05011v10.

[185] Rodriguez, A., Li, W., Dai, J., and Zhang, F., Intel® processors for deep learning training. Intel (17 November) [Online].

[186] Mulnix, D. (2017). Intel® Xeon® processor scalable family technical. Intel (10 July) [Online].

[187] AVX-512 Vector Neural Network Instructions (VNNI) – x86. WiKiChip - Chip & Semi [Online].

[188] (2018). Nvidia turing GPU architecture – graphics reinvented. Nvidia [Online].

[189] (2017). Nvidia Tesla P100 – the most advanced datacenter accelerator ever built featuring pascal GP100, the World's fastest GPU. Intel [Online].

[190] (2017). Nvidia Tesla V100 GPU architecture – the world's most advanced data center GPU. Nvidia [Online].

[191] Jouppl, N.P., Young, C., Patil, N., and Patterson, D. (2018). A domain-specific architecture for deep neural network. 18 September [Online].

[192] Jouppi, N.P., Young, C., Patil, N., and Patterson, D. (2018). A domain-specific architecture for deep neural networks. *Communications of the ACM* 61 (9): 50–59.

[193] Teich, P. (2018). Tearing apart google's TPU 3.0 AI processor. 10 May [Online].

[194] System architecture [Online]. http://cloud.google.com/tpu/docs/system-architecture.

[195] Patterson, D. (2019). Domain-specific architectures for deep neural networks. Google AI and UC Berkeley (April) [Online].

[196] Ward-Foxton, S. (2020). Kneron's next-gen AI SoC processes video and audio at the edge. *eetimes* (28 August) [Online].

[197] Kneron announces new generation edge AI processors NPU IP with up to 3x performance improvement to Hit 5.8 TOPS. Kneron [Online].

[198] Liu, A., Law, O., Chen, J.Y.C. et al. (2021). Traffic safety system edge AI computing. In *IEEE/ACM Symposium on Edge Computing (SEC), 2021*.

[199] https://www.kneron.com/

[200] https://git-scm.com/

[201] https://www.python.org/

[202] https://www.microsoft.com

[203] https://zadig.akeo.ie/

[204] https://ww.pytorch.org

[205] https://github.com/ultralytics/yolov5

Index

Understanding Artificial Intelligence: Fundamentals and Applications, First Edition.
Albert Chun Chen Liu, Oscar Ming Kin Law, and Iain Law.
© 2022 The Institute of Electrical and Electronics Engineers, Inc.
Published 2022 by John Wiley & Sons, Inc.

Printed and bound by CPI Group (UK) Ltd, Croydon, CR0 4YY

27/10/2024

14580668-0001